ACTIONABLE
PROFITABILITY
ANALYTICS

GOING BEYOND THE VISUALS
TO PRODUCE MEANINGFUL INSIGHTS
AND DRIVE PROFITABLE BEHAVIORS

ACTIONABLE
PROFITABILITY
ANALYTICS

SCOTT WISE

Printed in the United States of America.
ISBN: 978-1-949639-71-1

Cover design by Melanie Cloth.

To my wife, Jill—my beloved "partner in possibilities"—thank you for encouraging me to stop engineering smallness. I love you.

To my children—may your passions become your purpose and your endurance lead you to your expertise. Share it with the world.

To my clients, colleagues, and collaborators—all of you made this journey possible. This book represents our collective wisdom earned together from hard-fought project battles. Thank you.

To Micah—thank you for building a career as my "visioneer," you are a trusted partner and valued friend.

TABLE OF CONTENTS

INTRODUCTION

Numbers tell stories. They trumpet a business's triumphs. They expose weak spots and danger zones. They reveal so many stark truths, good and bad, about an organization. But are there other, potentially lucrative, stories buried in the balance sheet that the numbers might tell us?

The fact is that while a company's financial data provide a wealth of information, they also hold hidden secrets—unless you know where to look. Unless you know how to crack the code. Traditional accounting methods only reveal a partial picture of a company's performance. Profitability analytics is the oracle, the truth teller, the code breaker that crunches the reams of financial information from different facets in a large organization and spotlights novel, impactful ways of cutting costs and increasing profits.

If numbers tell the story of what's going on in a business, then profitability analytics look beyond surface-level accounting, peering deep down into the inner workings of a company to unveil the detail and nuance of the *economics* of the business itself. If accounting is focused on the basic "*what* happened," in terms of expenses and income, profitability analytics considers the "*why* it happened," by constructing a multidimensional view based on a broader set of variables and studying each variable on a granular level. It's powerful stuff.

By teaching you the fundamentals of profitability and cost analytics, this book will empower you to make crucial business decisions based on stronger evidence and a clearer set of criteria, instead of relying on inaccurate or inadequate data, anecdotal evidence, or gut feeling. We will go beyond the "eye candy" of visualizations, charting, and graphs of common business intelligence tools, and get under the hood of what it really takes to design, develop, and deploy actionable profitability analytics that produce meaningful insights and drive profitable behaviors.

Technologically, methodologically, and systematically, it's not an easy undertaking, but better analytics on the "economics of the business" *will* dramatically improve financial performance.

In the following pages, you'll gain a better understanding of how methodology, data, and technology come together to transform information to insight to impact. We will discuss the most challenging methodologies, the most common implementation challenges, and how to drive the most value to make the business case for these programs. These solutions are complex, requiring careful design, rigorous governance, and meticulous planning. Often, it's more art than science. You can't just plug-and-play the same set of formulas or let number-crunching software do all the heavy lifting. Rather, each case requires flexibility and problem-solving to apply the methods to an organization's unique business model and information demands. And even when you have an analytical program up and running, the challenge isn't over. These efforts are a journey and not a destination—continuous improvement and iteration are the keys to success.

While written primarily for CFOs, CIOs, and other leaders of Fortune 2000 companies, the principles and practices contained herein are applicable to a wide range of firms. Most of the examples you'll read about concern the financial services industry, but the lessons in this book are applicable to a number of other industries, too.

THE ARMADA STORY

Before I founded Armada, I was a consulting manager at one of the "Big Four" accounting firms. I excelled in and enjoyed my position, but I was working more as a generalist than a specialist—and what excited me the most was the niche specialization of profitability analytics, a challenging, enthralling field that I wanted to delve into more deeply. Rather than serving as a hired gun tackling different projects week to week and month to month, I was eager to focus only on this area. And I was starting to see the potential value of striking out on my own and building a new business around it.

The morning of September 11, 2001, I was in New Jersey for the week on a client site, while most of my team was at a financial services firm headquartered in New York City, where I was supposed to meet with my team later that day. When the first plane struck 1 WTC, I thankfully wasn't in the city and my team got out safely, but I was close enough to experience the upheaval of that day no American will ever forget. With air travel suspended coast-to-coast for two days, I had to drive back to Tulsa, where I reside and where Armada is now headquartered. There's nothing like a twenty-six-hour solo drive, in the aftermath of a national tragedy that had so many of us doing heavy soul-searching, to get your thoughts in order.

On those long hours on the highway, as the interstate unspooled beneath me, the first ideas for a new company dedicated to profitability analytics were laid down. Within six months, Armada Consulting was up and running, and since day one we've been building a reputation as a pioneer in the field. We've assembled a world-class team of professionals who have decades of collective experience in designing, developing, and deploying these types of analytics for some of the largest and most prestigious companies in the world.

Our razor-sharp focus and oceanic depth of experience are what make us unique. Most players in the analytics market rely on legacy applications built from decades-old methodologies, and they lack the flexibility to model the complexity of today's diverse organizations. Armada combines sophisticated proprietary technology with over two decades of hard-fought consulting and delivery expertise. We're not the only players in the industry, but I firmly believe we're the best—because this has been our sole focus since our inception. While other organizations might have a few professionals dealing with profitability analytics, or maybe a small division within a much larger firm, this is *all* we do, day in and day out. We work tirelessly on it at the office, and we think about it when we're at home. Sometimes, it even pops up in our dreams. (When I find myself dreaming about relationship pricing or strategic cost management, that's usually a good sign it's time for a vacation.)

In all seriousness, this intensive focus has allowed us to learn from our failures and successes as we continually refine our methodologies and technologies to generate solutions for unique, complex, and ever-changing challenges. It's not something everyone can do. It requires the right people with the right experience to succeed in this domain, but the reward can be immense for those willing to take on the challenge.

LOOKING AHEAD

The book is broadly divided into three sections, on value (Section I), methodology (Section II), and implementation (Section III). Chapter 1 introduces the idea of "actionable analytics" and provides an overview of how it works and who benefits. Chapter 2 looks at the advantages profitability analytics has over traditional accounting

(GAAP) methods. Chapter 3 highlights the value of transparency as the foundation of a strong analytics program.

In the second section, on methodology, Chapter 4 continues the discussion about transparency and links it to the all-important question of governance. Chapter 5 examines the multidimensional profitability analytics model, which provides detailed financial analytics across multiple dimensions. Chapter 6 teaches about strategic cost modeling, which allows a company to identify inefficiencies, unnecessary expenditures, and opportunities for cost takeout.

The final third of the book concerns implementation. Chapter 7 examines design and architecture, the solution blueprint to execute the profitability methodologies in a repeatable system. In Chapter 8, we examine how to assess your strengths and weaknesses as an organization as you get ready to roll out the program. Chapter 9 looks at deployment strategies and the ins and outs of navigating change. Finally, Chapter 10 concludes the book with a look toward how you can get started applying these ideas in your business and gain an edge over your competitors.

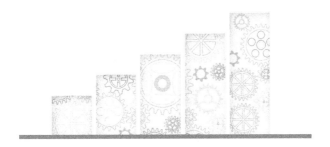

SECTION I

THE VALUE OF PROFITABILITY ANALYTICS

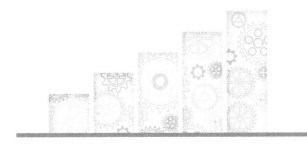

CHAPTER ONE
MORE THAN JUST NUMBERS: TAKING ACTION

What gets rewarded gets repeated, and what gets measured gets managed. Profitability analytics provides the measurement tools to look beyond the income statement of an organization to understand what happened, why it happened, and to provide insights on how to improve it. This permits businesses to strategically invest resources in areas that generate the biggest impact, while cutting costs with surgical precision.

Some years ago, a large regional bank contracted our firm to do a proof of value (POV) project. These are mini-projects where we zero in on one area of the organization, studying it closely to demonstrate how we can solve a specific problem, and then use that as a model for how we can bring value to the entire company.

The division this particular company chose for the POV project was plagued with high costs in some of its processing sites, and the executives were evaluating outsourcing proposals to bring costs in line. On the surface, it seemed that outsourcing was an attractive proposition. But one of the benefits of profitability and cost analytics is that it reveals solutions you otherwise wouldn't see—solutions you might not even know existed.

Our POV project served to demonstrate the value of deeper cost analytics, which provide the insight needed to make major decisions with confidence. We were going to have to show that the analytics value of our solution would pay for itself by exceeding the cost of implementation. The chief operating officer was already skeptical about our proposal. This was going to be a tough sell.

During the presentation, we unveiled a chart showing the breakdown of unit cost information for each of the company's nine processing sites, compared to the outsourcing bid. The outsourcing proposal would have achieved a cost reduction at two of the nine sites. We showed them that we could do better than that.

The real surprise came when we further broke down our analysis of the individual processing site costs by looking at the costs related to exception processes[1]. This was something the COO had not seen before. The chart showed that several of the sites had disproportionately high levels of non-standard processing, which accounted for the spike in costs. Our analysis reflected that if the company could eliminate the costs related to non-standard processing, six of the nine sites would be processing at a unit cost *below* the outsourced bid. Additionally, we were also able to identify the fixed cost structure that would not be eliminated through outsourcing.

---

1   "Non-standard processes" or "exception processes" are processes that deviate from how a given service is normally executed. For example, say a client is applying for a loan. Processing an application that is incomplete and requires soliciting more information from the client, or an application that needs expedited processing, would constitute a "non-standard process."

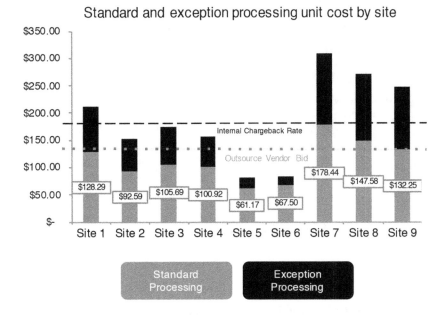

Ultimately, we were able to provide a much more granular level of detail that gave the executive team additional solutions, all backed by hard data. The prospective outsourcing option they had been considering would have been like using an axe to perform surgery. Instead, we gave them a scalpel.

Or, put another way—traditional accounting only gives you a 2D picture of what's happening. Profitability analytics is a 3D version. For the COO, watching our presentation was like putting on 3D glasses—finally, the image comes into focus and a level of depth and detail is revealed that you weren't able to see before.

The response was incredible. Minutes after leaving the room, the COO picked up the phone and called the executive of the division in question to say that they would not be outsourcing the operations group. Instead, she wanted to immediately start an improvement initiative to reduce the rate of non-standard processes within that business line. That initiative consisted of better training, better communication, improved standards of accountability, and internal benchmarking to compare the best performing sites against the worst. From information, to insight, to impact.

Ultimately, the proof of value project generated immediate, unmistakable value for the organization. We helped the company achieve five million dollars in annual savings, without the logistical and organizational burden of outsourcing. Six years later, they remain one of our most loyal clients.

LIGHTS, CAMERA, ACTION

It was after this experience that I began using the term "actionable profitability analytics" to describe our solution offerings—analytics that have immediate, powerful, and practical use; that provide clarity in decision making; and that generate a real and tangible impact for the business. Analytics that don't merely tell a story but give you the power to write your own—and usually, one with a happy ending.

Aggregated financial reporting, such as the income statement at the company level, only tells the story of *what* happened. The mysteries of why it happened are buried deep within that data. Actionable analytics provides answers to vexing questions such as: Who are our most and least profitable customers? How can we leverage that information effectively? What lines of business should we focus on to remain competitive? What business should we exit? What products and services require re-pricing to accommodate for increased costs? How do we better manage the primary levers of profitable growth?

Large, complex companies are composed of many departments and divisions that deal with a dizzying array of products and services sold across multiple channels to a variety of customers. Precisely calculating the actual cost and profit underlying so many variables is complex. Figuring out how to use that data to drive strategic decision making adds another wrinkle. Different dimensions interact with other dimensions: processes interface with technology, technology interacts with people, and products are delivered through diverse channels to customers in scattered geographic areas via different departments. To optimize your business model, you must disentangle all the moving parts to figure out a multitude of "who, what, where, and how" components. Analytics allows us to figure out which levers to pull and which buttons to push to optimize all these variables and maximize profit.

For example, if you're looking at things from an accounting perspective, you see a line item on the income statement that's marked "salaries." Normally, if you want to expand the bottom line by cutting back expenses, your only option would be to fire some people or to reduce the salaries of people in your employ. That's a rather heavy-handed and inelegant approach to a problem that could be resolved with more finesse, if you have the right tools.

Profitability analytics provides those tools. We would take that salary information and dig deeper to ask, "How do these salaries relate to the product or service that we're selling? What work activities are being performed by those people? What do those people cost? And how does that connect back to our salaries line in our accounting financials?" It means looking at the story *behind* the story of a single figure, like "salaries," to reveal the work that employees are performing, how it lines up with the services that are delivered, and how it relates to your sources of revenue.

We look at every dollar spent in the organization as an investment seeking a return, and we seek to align the expenses and costs of the organization to the revenue dollars that are generated from it.

You can't do that effectively from just the income statement at the total company.

TRIPLE THREAT

Another way of understanding actionable analytics is by breaking it down into its constituent components: methodology, technology, and data. Many companies specialize in one, or maybe two, of these areas. Hardly any of them are experts in all three. That's one of the things that makes Armada distinct—we occupy that exclusive sliver of real estate where methodology, technology, and data meet. Over the course of the book, we'll study how to cross-functionally manage all three.

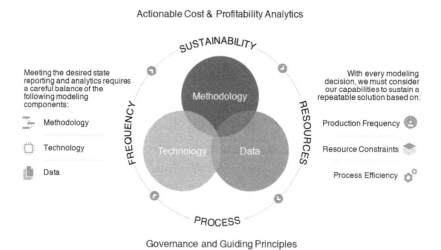

Actionable Cost & Profitability Analytics

Governance and Guiding Principles

Actionable analytics also enables executives to navigate the diffuse and often divergent agendas of various stakeholders within the organization—and make sure they're doing what they need to be doing. A product manager needs to understand what his or her fixed costs and variable costs are for delivering a certain product. A sales person might need to understand the details for marginal pricing decisions. A business executive is tasked with understanding the profitability of a specific line and needs to know how to hold people accountable so that they're meeting or exceeding performance targets. Everyone has their own responsibility, but sometimes, especially in large companies, it's easy to lose sight of who should be doing what and when.

The chart below, which divides stakeholders into three broad groups (operational management, business line management, and executive management), touches on this issue. All three groups are, ostensibly, working toward a common organizational goal, but as any manager knows, their individual interests—means of getting things done and sub-goals—sometimes conflict. Actionable analytics can help harmonize a disparate group of stakeholders by staying above the fray, looking at all the moving parts at a high level, in a way that allows for a strategic analysis of the data to drive better business decisions large and small. Now, instead of an organizational free-for-all, where every area brings their own analysis, it becomes easier to hold each stakeholder accountable when working with one consistent source of enterprise profitability analytics.

ENGAGING THE AUDIENCE ON PROFITABILITY ANALYTICS
Meeting the demands for analytics across diverse stakeholders

Operational Management
- Efficient and effective process delivery
- Optimize management of resource capacity
- Communicate the value they bring to organization

Business Line Management
- Optimize profitability of products and services
- Understand levers the can control to support profitable growth
- Analytics that enable smarter pricing decisions

Executive Management
- Improving global profitability and customer loyalty
- Protecting employee morale and commitment
- Credible financial performance data to optimize use of capital

As I said earlier, what gets rewarded gets repeated and what gets measured gets managed. As we'll see in later chapters, much of what makes profitability analytics work is its capacity to drill down through layers—of data, hierarchies, and complexity—to hold people accountable. How do we reward strong financial performance and disincentivize waste, inefficiency, and loss? How can we quantify a complex problem to know the right levers are being pulled and the right buttons pushed in the optimal combination to unleash the full force of the whole sprawling organization?

Everyone is going to take credit for a strong performance, and everyone will point a finger at someone else for a bad performance. The methods you will learn in this book break down the total company's financial performance into the specific areas that are contributing to, or detracting from, profitability. It helps to answer the question "Why?" and then drive the consequent action of, "What can we do about it?" In the next chapter, we'll examine why profitability analytics excels at this, while traditional accounting techniques fall short.

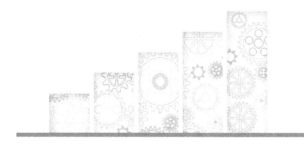

CHAPTER TWO

BRIDGING THE "GAAP": PROFITABILITY ANALYTICS VS. TRADITIONAL ACCOUNTING

Companies put a lot of emphasis on the financial performance of the organization from the outside, as measured by traditional accounting methods, but it's difficult to get a sense of internal performance—of the deep, inner workings of cost and profitability—with accounting alone. GAAP (Generally Accepted Accounting Principles) provides a flat, two-dimensional picture of a company's finances. Strategic profitability and cost analytics is multidimensional, allowing executives to understand the business from all angles. In other words, it reveals the *economics* of the business, illuminating much more detail than just the incursion of an expense or the receipt of revenue.

GAAP is well suited for providing comparatives *across* diverse companies with dissimilar business models. Profitability analytics provides information from an economic perspective *within* the company, allowing a multidimensional look across all products, customers, channels, processes, and organizational units in that company. In the same vein, the primary users of GAAP financial reporting are typically outside of the company, whereas the users of profitability analytics are typically within the company, seeking insights to improve financial performance.

Profitability analytics' power lies in its granularity. Imagine if you could get a potential P&L on every key dimension of your organization. That's the difference between this method and accounting. It expands the information value to be applicable in a broader context across a more diverse set of organizational stakeholders.

While profitability analytics has some key advantages over GAAP, that's not to say that one is designed to replace the other. Rather, the two must coexist and complement each other within the same organization. They are symbiotic; there is a place for both. But profitability analytics fulfills a role that accounting cannot.

FROM DIAGNOSIS TO CURE

In the traditional accounting view, your general ledger is restricted to what centers or business units you're accounting for and the accounting measures. You're measuring income from different sources and measuring elements like spending on people, buildings, sales, marketing, professional fees, and technology. Yet nowhere in that traditional accounting view does it tell you, "Who are my most and least profitable customers? Which products, geographies, or delivery channels earn the most money? For banks, how do we know that we make more profit from people who use online banking channels versus interacting with a teller at a branch?" We can even drill down to the level of individual customers:

"How much profit am I making from Joe Smith's loan? Or how much profit is generated by Joe's deposit account?"

We can make gut-feeling or anecdotal estimations about the profit and cost of these variables, but we need to be able to precisely *measure* them in order to make prudent, strategic, data-driven business decisions. Unlike GAAP, profitability analytics provides a window onto the minute, inner workings of customers, geographies, channels, products, services, and other factors, and how those variables interact multidimensionally. A Swiss watch is nice to look at from the outside, and it'll tell you the time, but you won't really understand how it works, or be able to appreciate its marvelous mechanics, until you can open it up and see how all the tiny, intricate gears mesh together to keep time accurately, down to the second.

When penetrating down into the intricate substrata of corporate financial performance, the limitations of accounting become quickly apparent. Profitability analytics goes beyond the GAAP view to shed light on the economics of the business model in play.

With profitability analytics, instead of simply talking about how we spent X dollars for the manager of Y branch, now (as illustrated in the left column of the following image), I can relate that figure to other variables: What does that provide my customer? What's the economic impact of that expense on the organization? We can get actionable answers to the kind of hyper-specific questions we've always wanted to ask.

Another key distinction between the two approaches is that accounting is more *retrospective* (looking at past performance) while profitability analytics is more *prospective* (looking ahead and thinking how to maximize future potential). With one approach, we're evaluating the past performance of the current business model. With the other, we're trying to identify opportunities to improve the economics of the future business model.

VIEWS OF CORPORATE FINANCIAL PERFORMANCE

Traditional Accounting View – Organizational Allocations

	Total Company	Front Office	Back Office
Income			
Interest Income / FTP Credits	$ xxx,xxx	$ xxx,xxx	
Interest Expense / FTP Charges	$ xxx,xxx	$ xxx,xxx	
Net Interest Margin	$ xxx,xxx	$ xxx,xxx	
Fee Income	$ xxx,xxx	$ xxx,xxx	
Total Income	$ xxx,xxx	$ xxx,xxx	
Direct Expenses			
Personnel	$ xxx,xxx	$ xxx,xxx	$ xxx,xxx
Sales & Marketing	$ xxx,xxx	$ xxx,xxx	$ xxx,xxx
Travel	$ xxx,xxx	$ xxx,xxx	$ xxx,xxx
Other	$ xxx,xxx	$ xxx,xxx	$ xxx,xxx
Total Direct Expense	$ xxx,xxx	$ xxx,xxx	$ xxx,xxx
Indirect Expenses			
Human Resources		$ xxx,xxx	($ xxx,xxx)
End User Computing		$ xxx,xxx	($ xxx,xxx)
Corporate Facilities		$ xxx,xxx	($ xxx,xxx)
Legal		$ xxx,xxx	($ xxx,xxx)
Finance		$ xxx,xxx	($ xxx,xxx)
Total Organizational Support Expenses		$ xxx,xxx	($ xxx,xxx)
Payment Operations		$ xxx,xxx	($ xxx,xxx)
Deposit Operations		$ xxx,xxx	($ xxx,xxx)
Risk Management		$ xxx,xxx	($ xxx,xxx)
Credit Underwriting		$ xxx,xxx	($ xxx,xxx)
Product Management & Marketing		$ xxx,xxx	($ xxx,xxx)
Customer Technology Applications		$ xxx,xxx	($ xxx,xxx)
Collections / Loss Mitigation		$ xxx,xxx	($ xxx,xxx)
Total Customer Support Expenses		$ xxx,xxx	($ xxx,xxx)
Corporate Security		$ xxx,xxx	($ xxx,xxx)
Line of Business Administration		$ xxx,xxx	($ xxx,xxx)
Regulatory / Investor Relations		$ xxx,xxx	($ xxx,xxx)
Brand Management		$ xxx,xxx	($ xxx,xxx)
Enterprise Sustaining Costs		$ xxx,xxx	($ xxx,xxx)
Total Business Sustaining Cost Allocations		$ xxx,xxx	($ xxx,xxx)
Total Expenses	$ xxx,xxx		
Net Income	$ xxx,xxx	$ xxx,xxx	$ 0

GL ACCOUNT I CENTER

VIEWS OF CORPORATE FINANCIAL PERFORMANCE

Strategic Economic View – Multidimensional Profitability

	Volume	Rate	Amount
Revenue			
Interest Income / FTP Credits			$ xxx,xxx
Interest Expense / FTP Charges			$ xxx,xxx
Net Interest Margin			$ xxx,xxx
Fee Income			$ xxx,xxx
Total Revenue			$ xxx,xxx
Consumption Based Customer Costs	Service Cost Detail		
Commercial Banking Sales	###	$ x.xx	$ xxx,xxx
Consumer Banking Sales	###	$ x.xx	$ xxx,xxx
Private Banking Sales	###	$ x.xx	$ xxx,xxx
Marketing	###	$ x.xx	$ xxx,xxx
Customer Acquisition Costs			$ xxx,xxx
Credit Underwriting Services	###	$ x.xx	$ xxx,xxx
Loan Operation Services	###	$ x.xx	$ xxx,xxx
Deposit Operation Services	###	$ x.xx	$ xxx,xxx
Account Origination Costs			$ xxx,xxx
Branch Banking Services	###	$ x.xx	$ xxx,xxx
Call Center Services	###	$ x.xx	$ xxx,xxx
Online Banking Services	###	$ x.xx	$ xxx,xxx
Product Maintenance Services	###	$ x.xx	$ xxx,xxx
Customer Relationship Mgmt Services	###	$ x.xx	$ xxx,xxx
Customer Servicing Costs			$ xxx,xxx
Teller Transactions	###	$ x.xx	$ xxx,xxx
Payment Transactions	###	$ x.xx	$ xxx,xxx
ATM Transactions	###	$ x.xx	$ xxx,xxx
Customer Transaction Costs			$ xxx,xxx
Total Customer Support Services			$ xxx,xxx
Loan Loss Provision			$ xxx,xxx
Risk Weighted Capital Charge			$ xxx,xxx
Total Risk Based Costs			$ xxx,xxx
Net Customer Profit Contribution			$ xxx,xxx
Business Sustaining Administrative Costs			
LOB Sustaining Costs			$ xxx,xxx
Regulatory / Investor Relations			$ xxx,xxx
Enterprise Sustaining Costs			$ xxx,xxx
Total Business Sustaining Cost Allocations			$ xxx,xxx
Economic Profit			$ xxx,xxx

ML ACCOUNT I CENTER I CUSTOMER I PRODUCT I BANKER

To use a medical analogy, think of the business like a doctor would deal with a patient. The doctor uses certain tests, indicators, and other diagnostic criteria to evaluate the patient's health. In that sense, both traditional accounting and profitability analytics are useful. But where accounting will reveal information about the symptoms, profitability analytics goes a step further—it points you toward a *cure*.

VIEWS OF CORPORATE FINANCIAL PERFORMANCE
Expanding the views of performance and profitability

	Traditional Accounting View		Strategic Economic View			
Time focus	Past Performance		Future Potential			
Perspective	External	Internal	Customer	Product	Channel	Process
Decision Support	Evaluates past performance of current Business Model		Identifies opportunities to improve economics of a future business model			
Users of Information	- Regulators - Shareholders - Tax Authority - Investors	- Board - LOB Execs - Controllers - Managers	- Sales - Marketing - Segment Mgmt - LOB Execs	- Product Mgmt - Marketing - Sales - LOB Execs	- Channel Mgmt - Branch Mgmt - Market Execs - LOB Execs	- Operations Mgmt - Process teams - LOB Execs
Reporting Level	Enterprise	Business Units	Customer Accounts	Product Portfolio	Delivery Channel	Process / Activity
Primary Output	- 10K & 10Q - Call Reports	- Org P&L	- Customer Profitability Statement	- Product Portfolio Profitability	- Channel Utilization	- Process Unit Costs
Measures Needed	Accounting	Financial	Financial · Operational · Market · Economic Value			
Governance	Regulatory and GAAP		Finance - Defines guiding principles specific to the organization			
System of Record	General Ledger		Instrument level profitability systems			

DRILLING DOWN TO THE SOURCE

All of this can seem very abstract, so let's consider a hypothetical. Say you're the head of a large national bank, and you want to determine which areas of the business are generating the most profit. Your company has thousands of customers, ranging from major corporate clients to retail-level account holders. There's a dizzying array of customers, channels, geographies, and divisions, and that complexity requires a powerful methodology to accurately tell you which areas are making money and which aren't.

The beauty of profitability analytics is that you can "zoom in" very closely to any face of the organization to obtain the desired information. For example, you can look at it from a product perspective. Ten thousand customers of your bank maintain a savings account. Profitability analytics permits you to group those savings accounts together and ask, "How much are we making on this particular product portfolio?"

You can break down the information into channels: Some of your clients bank online or on the phone, others visit branch locations and do their banking at the teller windows. Which produce the most profit at the least cost?

You can further break it down by processes or activities, such as in the story from the first chapter about the regional bank that was preparing to outsource one of its divisions. Strategic analytics can guide your decision making when it comes to nonstandard processing for a given service or product, and tell you what modifying or eliminating those processes would do to the overall profitability of the organization.

In addition, we can look at individual customer behavior. Say one of your account holders is Joe Smith, of Gary, Indiana. You can generate a specific profitability statement for Joe Smith that would show the profitability of his mortgage loan, his deposit account, his savings account, his credit card—all of the ways he does business with the company.

There are myriad ways of looking at the cost and profitability data of a large organization. The purpose of these analytics is an alignment of costs to revenue sources, in order to find ways to improve the business model.

It's important to remember that revenue has traceability to the customer account level, but costs require modeling. Expenses are incurred. Costs are derived. Expense is an accounting term. Cost is more of an economics term.

Calculating the revenue impact of a twenty-five-dollar overdraft fee is pretty straightforward. It's not so simple to compute the real *cost* of that overdraft, which is distributed over several different *expense* categories (labor costs for the person who has to process the overdraft, technology expenses, rent and facilities expenses). That information is not provided by accounting methods. Profitability analytics (specifically, strategic cost modeling, which is the subject of Chapter Six) lets us transform those expenses into meaningful costs or unit costs based on the product or service being provided.

If it sounds complicated, that's because it is. If it's not clear yet, I promise it will all become abundantly clear in the following chapters.

One of the exciting things about applying complex analytics to day-to-day business problems is that the results can defy expectations—things that seem intuitive or common-sense are revealed to be anything but. Anecdotal assumptions or gut-instinct guesswork can get you into trouble. Profitability analytics are good for exposing these blind spots and giving you objective data to make better business decisions.

For example, in banking, we spend an inordinate amount of time trying to get the doctors, the lawyers, the high-income people of the world to open accounts, based on the assumption that because they *earn* more, they're going to park all their money there and generate more revenue for the bank. On the surface, this makes sense. But on closer inspection, this is not necessarily the case. For instance, because they're high-income individuals, they're less likely to take out high-interest loans, and they're more likely to store their discretionary income in other investment offerings.

On the other end of the spectrum, you'll find low-income people; say, college students working part-time at the campus bookstore. It might seem unlikely that an underemployed undergrad would be a more profitable customer than a white-shoe lawyer or plastic surgeon, but often, the facts defy common sense.

Why? Well, once we start breaking down the unique consumer habits of individual customers, we might discover that even though that college student keeps a low monthly balance, they write several bad checks a month, and the overdraft fees generate a lot of profit for the bank. In this way, counterintuitively, such customers might make more desirable clients than the top-earning professionals.

That's why you need a more granular, three-dimensional analytic method to figure out what's what and who's who. Profitability and cost analytics elegantly smashes erroneous assumptions and supersedes anecdotal evidence by providing a laser-focused calculation of the true cost and profit of different variables.

So, if we know that certain customers produce certain revenue, and we know where the organization is spending money, how do we precisely connect the former with the latter, on a granular level? How can we model that in a clear and comprehensive way?

That's when the magic starts to happen, because when we begin modeling things that way, we get a three-dimensional picture of everything that happens within the organization: if it's a loan, what it costs to originate a loan; what activity, standard and nonstandard, originating that loan requires; what is the cost of the people or the technology or the outside services required to deliver that work; and so forth. In this way, we obtain valuable information that would otherwise remain invisible and which we can leverage to fine-tune pricing decisions, or to redesign and enhance products that better fit those particular segments that are driving the majority of our profitability.

COST & PROFITABILITY ANALYTICS
Modeling the 'economics of the business'

The key premise of cost modeling is to identify a traceable 'causal' relationship between customer choices and their expense impact

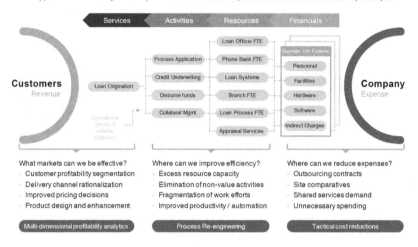

When we apply this type of analytics, we often see the Pareto principle, also known as the 80/20 rule, coming into play, in surprising ways. That's the principle, observed in economics, in sociology, even in nature, that holds that 80 percent of effects are produced by 20 percent of the cause. In business, this means that 20 percent of your customers might generate 80 percent of profits—or 20 percent of your clients account for 80 of costs. Understanding this radically uneven distribution of cost and profit enables businesses to focus on the most profitable sectors and de-emphasize or cut out the ones that are a drag on the organization's performance.

When you line up costs specific to revenue sources, you can start to spot outliers and bolster efficiency and productivity. That kind of strategic clairvoyance isn't provided by the aggregated financials of traditional accounting methods.

BE THE CAPTAIN OF YOUR SHIP: LOOKING OFF THE FRONT OF THE BOAT

Once we have that understanding of what, specifically, it takes to serve our clients, then we can start looking off the front of the boat. We can plan more precisely for the future.

Accounting, as I said earlier, is more retrospective—looking off the back of the boat, examining where we've already been. Profitability analytics directs our gaze to where we're going in terms of markets, geographies, channels, and even individual customers. Now that we have data that reveal who are our most and least profitable customers, we can start to forecast what they'll do in the future. We can model more predictive information around a customer's lifetime value.

Let's revisit our previous example about the hapless college kid who keeps getting hit with those overdraft charges. He might be writing bad checks now, but in a couple years he'll graduate and enter the workforce; a year after that he'll take out a loan for a fancy car; in five years he'll put a down payment on his first house; and a few years after that he'll get married and start saving long-term for his family and investing in his retirement.

Therefore, even if he's writing bad checks now, at age twenty-one, he has in front of him a whole lifetime of financial engagement with the bank, and if we can adequately analyze the projected financials of this customer and other customers like him, we can start to model out customer lifetime value and rethink our future business strategy. It's difficult to get down to that level of precision, but if you can achieve it, you gain an enormous competitive advantage.

Strategic profitability analytics keeps you abreast of the micro- and macro-trends that keep you profitable. Business is changing. Consumer behavior is changing. Society itself is changing. You can see that happening today with branch banking, which has fallen out of favor among younger generations of customers who do their banking at home or on their mobile device.

Consequently, banks are studying these changes and adapting their service delivery to keep pace. That means shifting resources to digital platforms, while reconfiguring the bank-branch model itself. That's why some branch locations that have looked more or less the same for thirty years have starting adopting a trendy "coffeehouse" aesthetic to attract younger customers.

The point is not that the "new" way is automatically better than the "old" way, or that companies should always be chasing the consuming trends of the day. Rather, the point is that you need a systematic, data-driven method to *know* what works and what doesn't—something that tells you which way the winds are blowing, so that you can steer your boat where it needs to go.

E PLURIBUS UNUM: OUT OF MANY, ONE

Within a large organization, there is a panoply of different stakeholders who need particular information around cost and profitability. Serving all of them is one of the challenges of doing actionable analytics right, since there's no blanket, cookie-cutter, or plug-and-play solution. Each problem demands its own careful analysis, and each stakeholder uses that information is unique ways to get the answers they need to do business. But even though the applications vary, everyone is drawing water from the same well in order to provide a consistent, cohesive source of data with which to make key business decisions.

Without profitability analytics, each stakeholder is generating their own information—essentially, creating their own version of the truth as they clamor for their share of organizational resources. It's like a room full of heads of state and they're all speaking different languages—at best, things get lost in translation. At worst, you get World War III.

The solution is to consolidate a company's financial information in one centrally governed source of analytics and model that data out using the same methodology, so that everybody's seeing the same data points and reacting appropriately. That's one of the challenges we'll discuss in the next chapter.

CHAPTER THREE
ONE TRANSPARENT, CENTRALLY GOVERNED SOURCE

In one of my first jobs in this field, I was helping a bank deal with some cost-allocation issues. Its HR costs were running pretty high, and we were looking at creative ways to trim expenses and make the company more profitable.

In any company, you can look at "HR costs" as the expenditures incurred by the human resources department, but you can also think of HR costs as distributed throughout the whole organization, since all departments and divisions consume HR services in one way or another. The bank that had contracted me calculated the HR costs of each of its four major divisions based on FTE (full-time equivalents)—a fancy term for "number of employees." That might *seem* like a reasonable cost-allocation basis. Human resources deals with people, and so the HR costs for each division were simply a function of the number of people employed in each division.

However, as this case shows, even if methods of figuring out cost and profit are logical or fair, they aren't necessarily *transparent*. And if it's not transparent, then it's hard to really get a sense of what's going on under the hood. The FTE allocation method told the company how many HR dollars were spent per employee, but it didn't reveal anything about why or how all those dollars were being spent. They needed a better way of looking at cost allocation, and that's where Armada stepped up to the plate.

To get more transparent information, we had to look more closely at the services HR was providing. Generally speaking, HR does a few things. They make sure people get paid. They manage workplace policies and procedures. They conduct training programs. They handle recruitment and hiring. What we wanted to figure out was the *economic impact* of those different functions on the company as a whole, and on the different divisions in particular.

In any organization, certain divisions are going to consume more resources (including HR resources) than other divisions. Faulty allocation processes can create a subsidization across multiple organization units—one entity ends up indirectly paying for the services of another. And certain divisions are allocated more dollars simply because they have more people, without regard to their actual consumption. Breaking all this data down into not just FTE, but economic drivers, gives you more transparent information to make better business decisions.

In this bank, the HR function was distributed across the company's four major departments: a commercial banking division, a consumer banking division, wealth management, and the operations groups. The commercial and the consumer divisions had about the same number of total staff, but the consumer division had a high employee-turnover rate, and consequently, they were leaning hard on

HR for help with recruitment, retention, and training. This meant that their HR "consumption" was higher, even though it had as many employees as its counterpart.

Once I started developing a more transparent picture of how the HR allocation dollars were moving through the organization, it became clear that the consumer division was getting less than what it should have, and the commercial division was receiving more than its fair share. Put another way, the commercial line of business was subsidizing the consumer line of business through misappropriated cost allocations when done on a purely FTE basis.

The goal of having financial transparency is that the users of this information can do something with it. *Actionable* analytics depends on usable data. Once we showed the company that high HR costs in the consumer division were due to high turnover, they implemented measures to improve retention and recruiting, and they collaboratively worked together to manage the demand for these HR services, instead of simply reducing HR staff.

That's what financial transparency gets you: It provides clarity into what's really going on in the business and empowers leaders to make better, fact-based decisions that drive profitable behavior.

THE TRUTH (AND NOTHING BUT THE TRUTH...)

Profitability analytics doesn't actually work unless the stakeholders have faith in the data being used. Transparency in the analytics creates one version of the truth on which everyone can rely.

A lack of transparency, in contrast, leads to misguided strategy and bad decisions. It weakens the underlying data used to allocate resources and make decisions, and it produces subsidizations and bickering between departments. It creates a situation where every stakeholder (every department, division, decision-maker, etc.) will bring to the table different financial data analyzed using different rules or methodologies, and everyone will be shouting over each other in an attempt to advance their own agenda.

While small firms may struggle with transparency, the problem mostly afflicts large, diverse companies, as one might expect. In the big organizations, the vast diversity of product and service offerings, workforce, hiring procedures, channels and markets, and everything else makes it extremely difficult to provide any level of transparency beyond just general accounting.

In these companies, so much time and effort is spent on breaking down accounting information to provide insights, with each analysis having a different basis for measurement. This causes confusion and produces contradictory information. Establishing a centrally governed framework for profitability analytics ensures that certain guiding principles are used across all of the analytics. Similar to GAAP for external reporting, it ensures that the resulting information is comparable and credible, and fit for use in decision making, removing any bias or assumptions, and treating all elements on an equitable basis. Only when this is done can you really make rational, informed, strategic decisions.

TRANSPARENCY = FLEXIBILITY

The more robust and transparent your data, the more flexible you can be in your decision making, since the improved quality of information allows you to see problems from a different angle and come up with a broader range of solutions.

If you only have the accounting view of the world—looking at specific expense line items, like "personnel expenses," instead of considering the underlying economics involved—it limits the range of your decision making, since in that case, the only real remedy is, "I can hire more people, or I can lay some people off."

Well, firing some people might achieve the desired goal of reducing personnel expenses, but what about the downstream impact on other parts of the organization? If laying people off has an adverse effect on product and service quality, on customer satisfaction, on morale, on all kinds of things that affect profitability, then the "solution" becomes self-negating. That's the limitation of GAAP accounting.

Profitability analytics expands your arsenal with a more powerful weapon—a sniper rifle, rather than a shotgun. Transparent data is like the ammo loaded into that sniper rifle. It gives you more options to solve vexing business problems with surgical precision, instead of blunt-force, heavy-handed methods of cost reduction, such as, "Everybody's got to cut their expenses by 10 percent across the board." Good, transparent data, from one unified source, tells you, "Here are the areas that are underperforming. Here are the root causes of those costs. And here's how we can improve." Just as in the case of the bank that I discussed at the start of the chapter, once that data provided us insight into the *causes* of those costs, we were in a position to help the company change their practices to decrease turnover, and thus reduce expenditures for recruiting. In the end, it wasn't just an HR problem. Strategic changes in one division had a positive downstream effect on others.

Another situation in which subsidization commonly occurs is within the IT department in large firms. IT is a high-cost part of any organization, and every division within the organization is going to use IT services. But if you allocate all of your technology resources on a "flat rate" basis of X dollars per employee, you're going to have an uneven distribution, since of course not everyone consumes IT services equally. Not only that, but you might end up incentivizing wasteful spending—if costs aren't aligned with consumption, then everyone's going to request two iPhones, or two monitors, and there's no real disincentive against doing so.

It would be the equivalent of a supermarket that, instead of simply pricing products individually based on their market value, charged customers a flat $150-per-week to come in and grab any items of their choice. It's not hard to imagine what would happen in this ill-advised scenario: People would fill their carts with nice cuts of meat, twelve-year-old scotch, and other top-shelf goods, leaving all the ramen noodles and tinned sardines on the shelves. What gets rewarded gets repeated.

And to be clear, when we talk about cost transparency, we're not just talking about employees using organizational resources. Transparency also applies to figuring out the real costs of consumer behaviors. For example, say every checking account holder of a bank pays ten dollars a month to maintain their account. Not all customers are created equal. Customers who write and cash checks and interact with a teller ten times a month consume services differently from the account holder who does all their transactions automatically and electronically. You've got to drill down and understand the economic impact of these distinct behaviors.

Therefore, whether we're talking about the cost of the services provided internally to the organization's employees, or the cost of the services provided to the customers the organization serves, the goal is the same: to align costs with revenue in order to make better business decisions informed by clear and accurate data.

FROM INFORMATION TO INSIGHT

At the end of the day, profitability analytics is designed to properly align and measure the financial performance of your customers, your products, your services, and your business units. Yet not all customers, not all business units, and not all revenue or expense dollars are created equal. Without transparency, you don't have the means to understand how all these variables and dimensions interact. You don't have a way to figure out which parts of the company are generating the most profit.

Transparency goes hand in hand with governance—ensuring everyone is playing by the same rules while holding leaders and departments within the firm accountable for their financial performance. Transparency is essential for governance because it creates one centrally administered source of information. In a large, multifaceted organization, this ensures that everything is done fairly and equitably across the board. Instead of ten managers coming to the table with ten competing analytic methods (and thus ten different versions of the truth), everyone stays on the same page. Everyone speaks the same language.

Section II will dive into questions of governance and methodology. Governance provides the framework, or scaffolding, to facilitate the difficult undertaking of profitability analytics. Without transparency, you can't have governance, and without governance, no methodology is going to work.

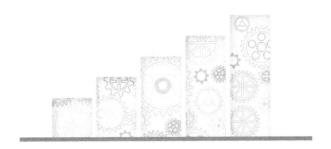

SECTION II
A METHODOLOGY TO THE MADNESS

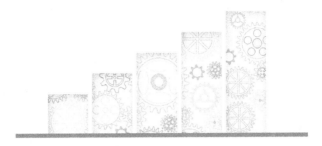

CHAPTER FOUR
GUIDELINES AND GUARDRAILS

Unlike GAAP, profitability analytics do not have established standards for how to model the financials of the organization and provide performance-management reporting within the organization. Each company must adopt its own set of guiding principles that shape the management accounting methodologies they want to adhere to. This is more art than science, as each organization is different; each one has its own set of challenges and goals.

Hence, in profitability analytics, there is no one-size-fits-all approach. There's not even a "one-size-fits-two-or-three." Every situation is unique.

One organization may seek to change the way they measure profitability across different dimensions to develop a better incentive compensation plan. Another organization may want to go really deep into operational activity to perform cost takeout or explore an outsourcing. Another might be looking at product re-pricing or new customer segments. Whatever the problem at hand, the methodology must be guided by the specific business goal—what is the desired outcome from these analytics? What behavior is incented? Will the analytics provided drive strategic profitable growth? That's where everything starts.

GUIDING PRINCIPLES LAY THE FOUNDATION

Developing a profitability-analytics program first requires establishing a set of "guiding principles." Guiding principles and methodology are related, and they depend on one another, but they're not the same thing. Guiding principles *precede* methodology; they set the framework for the right methodology to emerge.

Guiding principles:

- Set initial direction and identify key items for discussion,

- establish clear "rules of engagement" between business units,

- translate strategic objectives into measurement methodology,

- address key methodology debates early in the process rather than later,

- identify issues which may require senior management decisions,

- ensure consistent application of methodologies before results are measured,

- overall, help to ensure program success.

By defining the business objectives an organization is pursuing, guiding principles help answer several key questions related to methodology:

- What behaviors do you want to influence through profit-ability analytics?

- Who will be the audience or stakeholders of the information?

- How will the analytics be leveraged throughout the enterprise?

- Why were certain measurement methodologies deployed?

- When is it appropriate to change methodologies and models?

They specify the data you need, the technology you're going to use, the reporting protocols required, the methodology to execute the process, and the implementation plan that will bring everything into reality.

For example, a guiding principle might say, "We want to measure customer profitability on a consumption basis—based on the economics behind the customer's behavior. In other words, measuring a customer's performance based on the things that they do, not just allocate costs."

That's a clear, well-defined goal. Once the major stakeholders are in agreement on that point, they can move forward and think about methodology, which in this case, might be a consumption-based cost methodology that applies a standard unit cost rate to the volume of consumption, instead of a monthly allocation of actuals from supporting business areas.

The point is that the *methodology* (figuring out costs based on consumption) derives from the *guiding principle* that (in this example) we want to be able to measure the difference between the economic impact of individual customers, based on their different consumption behaviors around the same product or service.

Conversely, a guiding principal might state, "We want to reflect actual monthly expenses out to the customers, on a fair and reasonable basis, and not incur the measurement costs associated with customer volume collection." This principal might forge a different methodological path: Not a consumption-based cost methodology but an allocation methodology.

A guiding principal *guides* the project team into establishing the right methodology, data, and technology to meet the target-state solution. Setting the guiding principles is the first step in every profitability program, and provides the foundation for a sustainable solution.

Example Guiding Principle

Guiding Principle	Rationale
Consumption Based Cost Methodology The majority of costs should be recovered on a consumption basis reflecting the causal economic relationship between providers and receivers. The cost methodology will minimize arbitrary allocations of expenses, in favor of consumption based cost recovery.	- Defining standard unit cost rates annually is a leading practice to remove expense seasonality and provide predictable costs for pricing, planning and profit analytics - Methodology engages providers and receivers in cost control dialog grounded in the economic relationship between the activities performed and consumer behavior - Monthly updates of unit cost rates would be unsustainable within cost team resource constraints

	Implications
All organizations will calculate annual standard unit costs for services delivered and recover these costs based on actual monthly volumes of consumption Business sustaining organizations with costs that have no direct causal relationship will be allocated on a fair and reasonable basis determined by finance.	- Increased dependency on quality volume data by receiving dimensions of organizations or customers - Providers are accountable for lowering unit cost, receivers accountable for managing consumption volume - Use of standard unit cost methodology will result in a residual variance to monthly actual expenses that will require further allocation

Generally, the top five guiding principles I like to establish at the onset of each engagement address the following:

- **Economic-based principles**: Gain commitment and set parameters around modeling profitability data based on the economics of the business rather than the accounting.

Define upfront the measures that drive actionable analytics and any deviations from GAAP accounting principles.

- **Cost variability**: Achieve consensus on how to manage and report fixed versus variable costs and address actions or behaviors that will result from having that transparency.

- **Materiality**: What is material to the mission, and what is not? What are the material strategic measures we need to advance? This means avoiding "boiling the ocean" with meaningless minutiae. What is an actionable strategic level of materiality, that ensures "the view is worth the climb."

- **Sustainability**: Establish a means to keep the program sustainable over the long term within the resource constraints of the organization. Aim high, but don't bite off more than you can chew. The goal is to think big, start small, and deliver incremental value.

- **Consumption-based cost methodology**: Define upfront to avoid subjective allocations of expense and adopt a consumption-based cost methodology based on standard unit costs that remain consistent annually, and are recovered against actual volumes consumed. Limit subjective monthly allocations of actual expenses to drive more credible profitability analytics.

Naturally, all these principles don't magically appear on your desk one day, out of thin air. Human beings—yes, that means you—need to think forward to the possible outcomes and get executives to agree on them, together, and in advance of implementation. Since many stakeholders are involved in the project, it requires a working committee or steering committee to hammer out the guiding principles. This program governance gives every person a voice and adds some measure of procedure, decorum, and organization to what would otherwise be a messy process. The committee should be representative of all the business units that have a stake and should fluidly crisscross the different lines of business. In this way, you achieve buy-in and executive ownership of the program and help ensure that it's integrated with the company as a whole.

In addition to defining business goals and influencing methodology, guiding principles also allow the analytics project team to operate freely, without having to go and ask the executive team for direction or permission on every individual issue they come across. The team can operate with established, agreed upon rules that let them go in and do the work they need to do without getting hung up on last minute questions about process and procedure.

And that's good governance, in essence—creating a set of rules to facilitate a program, and ensuring that everyone plays by those rules. Achieving everything expediently and efficiently, so you don't need to create a process for every little situation that might arise. Governance is essential for upfront planning, securing the necessary resources, achieving agreement on methodologies, defining roles and responsibilities, and setting up a solid implementation framework. Otherwise, the wheels are going to come off as soon as you move out of the gate.

ESTABLISHING STAKEHOLDER GOVERNANCE

Typical Performance and Profitability program structure

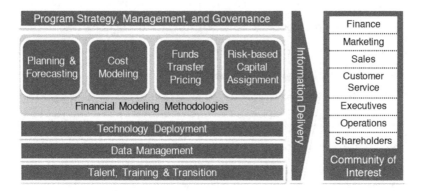

Planning, committed resources, defined roles and responsibilities and a solid implementation framework are keys to successful deployment

SPEAKING OF WHEELS—THE SQUEAKY ONE GETS THE GREASE

When you're doing strategic planning or performance management in a large organization with multiple lines of business, every department is clamoring to be heard and everyone has a reason for why their line of business is the most profitable or most essential to the company's future. Basically, every divisional leader within the company sees their division, department, or branch as their baby—and no one likes to be told their baby is ugly.

So when it comes to actually figuring out who is right about their unit's success, the one who wins the argument is usually just the loudest voice in the room. Maybe it's the guy with the snazziest PowerPoint. Maybe it's the team that happens to excel at touting their achievements in meetings. The criteria become very subjective. But we need objective, merit-based ways of evaluating performance and profitability from one centrally governed source of analytics. And in the absence of good governance, guiding principles, and a strong methodology, everyone comes to the table with their own analysis of their line of the business's performance. It's not even necessarily that they're fudging numbers or embellishing their success, it's just that there's rarely a credible, centralized version of the truth to objectively measure performance within these large organizations.

In such situations, this is where Armada steps in and breaks through the gridlock by uniting all the warring factions under one common purpose, driven by an objective set of criteria that will answer these questions about who's most profitable and least profitable. Because after all, corporate leaders, deep down, don't *want* to argue with each other (well, most of 'em). They want the whole enterprise to thrive, not just their part of it.

That's also one of the things that distinguishes Armada's approach. We don't merely come in and say, "We're going to build you an analytics system. Tell us what you want." We help companies step back, take a clear-eyed look at their organizational goals, and then tell us about the business outcomes they're trying to achieve. Then, before we look at a single piece of data, we assist them in establishing guiding principles that everyone across the organization agrees on for how we're going to measure profitability, measure costs, and pull all this together.

This is all established upfront, with the blessing of all the stakeholders, so that when we finish modeling the organization's financials and the profitability numbers come in, those stakeholders can't sit there and debate the results or attack the methodologies because the numbers didn't work in their favor. They're beholden to the principles that they and everyone else agreed on in the beginning.

CASE STUDY: THE GOOD

Establishing a foundation of good governance and clear guiding principles makes everything run smoothly, as exemplified by one of our clients, a major US bank, whose project ended up being one of our speediest and most successful implementations. This company had not done any work in cost and profitability analytics, but they came to us with a very clear objective: they wanted to change their incentive compensation so that it would be based on the profitability of each individual customer account.

Most sales commissions systems are based on how much revenue a salesperson generates. More revenue means more money coming in, so the salesperson should be duly rewarded on the assumption that more revenue equals better performance, right? But it's not always so simple. With profitability analytics, there is more than meets the eye. There's almost always another story hidden beneath the surface.

Tying commissions to revenue is not always optimal because it might incentivize the wrong kind of behavior. You can have a salesperson who's netting a ton of revenue, but the customers they're bringing on board aren't actually profitable.

Our client company had a hunch this was the problem, but it was just that, a hunch—they didn't have the hard numbers to prove it, and, more importantly, they lacked the analytic capacity to devise a better system in which incentive compensation is based on the customers' risk-adjusted profitability.

That's where we came in.

Once we helped the company change the carrot at the end of the stick to be *profitability* rather than *revenue*, it had a downstream effect on the day-to-day behavior of the sales personnel, who were now focused on finding better and more profitable customers.

In this case, the key was starting with a clear objective codified in strong guiding principles. That's the seed of a successful analytics project. A clear objective bears fruit: explicit expectations, a decisive strategy, and an appropriate methodology to support it. After all, in order to figure out what you need to do, you have to know where it is you want to end up.

CASE STUDY: THE BAD

Then you have the guys who seem to get it wrong from the very beginning, plunging the project into a whole mess of complications and crises that could have been avoided with a bit of forethought and level-headed discussion. It's imperative to start any profitability-analytics program by creating a working committee that will establish the guiding principles. One large banking organization we worked with had failed to do this. And this oversight showed in the results.

The organization had recently undergone a major realignment, during which they had centralized all the operations of the mortgage division within a massive shared services organization within the company. We spent nine months modeling the cost and profitability of the shared services and operations group. And once the mortgage operations had been integrated with the service organization, we did what's called "shared services chargeback," where in essence, we had to calculate the costs of all the mortgage service operations (originating a new housing loan, maintaining a mortgage account, etc.) now that these services were performed under the umbrella of shared services. Then we assigned those costs out to the mortgage division where the revenue resided.

Well, once we figured out the costs, the mortgage division leaders were *furious* because all of a sudden, the costs they received were greater than the expenses of the operations group they trans-ferred to the centralized services division. Costs had risen on paper, since now the modeling had to account for the extra overhead of the shared services division. When the mortgage services had been an independent line of business, it cost them, say, $4,000 to originate a mortgage, but now that they had shifted it over to the services company (which had to tack on its own overhead costs), what before cost $4,000 now cost $5,000.

The problem was not that the estimated costs were inaccurate, but that they had no common guiding principles across the various divisions, each of which was calculating things according to its own methodology. They had no unifying method of dealing with overhead within these different, expansive lines of business that comprised the shared services group. And so for the mortgage department, those costs seemed to go up.

Guiding principles serve as the voice of reason, the calm, stoic leader or fair, impartial judge who gives direction to a room full of disagreeing executives. But when those principles are not in place, as was the case with this bank, what happens is the head of the business unit that is suddenly laden with unforeseen costs kicks and screams until the CEO says, "Okay, fine, we won't charge $5,000 for each loan origination; we're going to charge $4000 like before," in an arbitrary effort to appease the exec screaming his head off. And that's what happened at this bank. But that move was just sweeping the problem under the rug, since all it did was shift the extra $1,000 dollars per unit of overhead to some other line of business.

It's the kind of kick-the-can short-term fix that produces long-term problems down the road—bad for a business of any size.

Of course, this debacle could have been avoided. Before the bank undertook the integration of the mortgage division within the

ACTIONABLE PROFITABILITY ANALYTICS

shared services organization, all the stakeholders should have set up guiding principles, which would have created a plan for dealing with the problem of "sudden" extra costs.

Eventually, the executives did rectify the situation by going back, working out the guiding principles in hindsight, and applying them from that point forward. But the credibility of the cost methods were tainted, and it's hard to come back from that.

Obviously, whether you're putting together a new set of cabinets on Saturday afternoon, or realigning whole divisions within one of the largest banking organizations in the world, it's better, and vastly easier for everyone, to do things right ahead of time rather than patching over problems retroactively.

CASE STUDY: ... AND THE UGLY

Here's another cautionary tale. We lost a bid to another firm, since our plan predicted higher costs in the design and governance phase than our competitor's bid. The competitor firm started their project by dropping off a busload of consultants to immediately start executing and building a system, without doing the recommended design and governance phase and without defining clear guiding principles. Eventually, the company realized they had erred and called us back in to right the ship. But the damage was done: months of wasted work and hundreds of thousands of dollars down the drain.

Because of its complex, case-by-case nature, profitability analytics defies standardization. It's more art than science. Every application is different. That's why devising the right methodology is so critical. And that's why good governance and guiding principles are an indispensable starting point. They provide the guardrails.

This kind of analytics is a powerful machine—a souped-up 1968 Shelby Mustang let loose on the asphalt. It'll get you to your destination fast and in style. But skipping (or skimping on) guiding principles is like taking that three-hundred-horsepower muscle car on a twisting, winding mountainside road with no guardrails separating you from the ravine on the other side.

If a company tries to forge ahead without good governance and the right methodologies, they'll quickly find their goals don't align with the solutions.

Fortunately, now you understand how to avoid that trap. The next two chapters will delve more deeply into the two primary components of actionable profitability analytics: multidimensional profitability analytics, and strategic cost modeling.

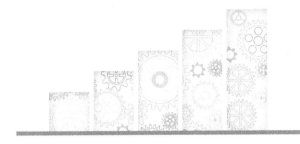

CHAPTER FIVE

MULTIDIMENSIONAL PROFITABILITY ANALYTICS DEFINED

Multidimensional profitability analytics is the ability to measure profitability from any dimension in the business, while ensuring that it all reconciles back to the overall financials of an organization. Think of it like a Rubik's Cube, where each dimension's data is a different color on the cube, and all the colors are mixed up. To solve the puzzle, you want to align all the colored squares to get a clear, cohesive, ordered picture—the equivalent of aligning different sources of data to pinpoint where the most profitable segments of the business are thriving, and where the least profitable ones are holding back the pack.

The goal of profitability analytics is to be able to establish a common set of profitability measures for any dimension in the business. A dimension can mean a certain product, a business unit or organization, a particular customer, a specific salesperson, a certain geography, and so forth. Multidimensional profitability analytics basically pulls that information together so that you can slice and dice your performance and profitability information in a number of different ways—on the same set of metrics applicable to all dimensions. The value of this is obvious: Finally, you *can* compare apples to oranges (and apples to pears, strawberries, carrots, and potatoes—any dimension).

The insight that profitability analytics provides into the economics of a business drives better strategic decisions involving product repricing, understanding who are your most and least profitable customers, understanding how a particular business unit or organization is performing, and a host of other concerns. It is the methodology that lets us build one central source of the truth around performance and profitability data. For example, let's look at the economics of the banking business in the following diagram.

A bank serves customers across multiple market areas through various products (loans, checking accounts, etc.), in which they provide value to those customers through services delivered through various channels. In the delivery of those services, the bank deploys resources (people, systems, etc.) that incur expenses within various organizations or centers within the bank. Also, the bank has organizational support centers (HR, technology, and so forth) that serve the needs of the customer-facing organizations with support services (such as training or applications) to enable the delivery of value to the bank's customers. The bank's customers provide revenue in the form of interest income and fee income to the bank for these value-added services.

The difference between the revenue and costs, as any freshman business student understands, is profit. When looking at the organization in its entirety and at the corporate level, accounting does a good job of telling us that net income or profit number in aggregate.

Modeling the customer value chain across primary profitability dimensions

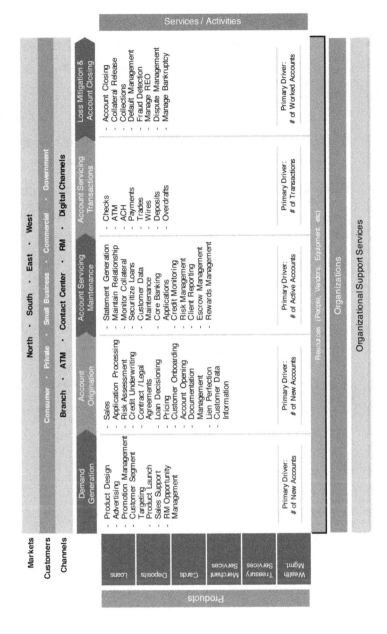

Markets North · South · East · West

Customers Consumer · Private · Small Business · Commercial · Government

Channels Branch · ATM · Contact Center · RM · Digital Channels

Services / Activities

Demand Generation
- Product Design
- Advertising
- Promotion Management
- Customer Segment
- Targeting
- Product Launch
- Sales Support
- RM Opportunity Management

Primary Driver: # of New Accounts

Account Origination
- Sales
- Application Processing
- Risk Assessment
- Credit Underwriting
- Contract / Legal Agreements
- Loan Decisioning
- Pricing
- Customer Onboarding
- Account Opening
- Documentation Management
- Lien Perfection
- Customer Data Information

Primary Driver: # of New Accounts

Account Servicing Maintenance
- Statement Generation
- Maintain Relationship
- Monitor Collateral
- Securitize Loans
- Customer Data Maintenance
- Core Banking Applications
- Credit Monitoring
- Risk Management
- Client Reporting
- Escrow Management
- Rewards Management

Primary Driver: # of Active Accounts

Account Servicing Transactions
- Checks
- ATM
- ACH
- Payments
- Trades
- Wires
- Deposits
- Overdrafts

Primary Driver: # of Transactions

Loss Mitigation & Account Closing
- Account Closing
- Collateral Release
- Collections
- Default Management
- Fraud Detection
- Manage REO
- Dispute Management
- Manage Bankruptcy

Primary Driver: # of Worked Accounts

Resources (People, Vendors, Equipment, etc)

Organizations

Organizational Support Services

Products
- Loans
- Deposits
- Cards
- Merchant Services
- Treasury Services
- Wealth Mgmt

Not all revenue dollars generate the same profit dollars. The goal for multidimensional profitability analytics is to identify the profit at the intersection of the dimensions of this economic model. Then we can gain insights into the most and least profitable aspects of our business. Through these analytics we can establish a common set of profit measures that provide actionable information on the economics of the business, not simply the accounting.

The following figure shows an example of a multidimensional P&L that standardizes the profitability statement across dimensions. For this banking industry example, the components and sources of that data are:

- Revenue and Balances

  □ Sourced from customer account detail

- Cost of Funding

  □ FTP Charges and Credits at account level

- Cost of Capital

  □ Economic Capital at account level

  □ Capital charge calculations

- Cost to Serve

  □ Consumption Based Cost Assignments

    □ Standard Unit Cost * Volume

  □ Business Sustaining Costs

    □ Allocation of business sustaining costs

Multidimensional Profitability Statement

	Volume	Rate	Amount
Revenue			
Interest Income / FTP			
Credits			$ xxx,xxx
Interest Expense / FTP			
Charges			$ xxx,xxx
Net Interest Margin			$ xxx,xxx
Fee Income			$ xxx,xxx
Total Revenue			$ xxx,xxx
Consumption Based Costs			
Customer Acquistion Costs	####	$ x.xxx	$ xxx,xxx
Channel / Delivery Costs	####	$ x.xxx	$ xxx,xxx
Product Support Costs	####	$ x.xxx	$ xxx,xxx
Transaction Costs	####	$ x.xxx	$ xxx,xxx
Total Cost to Serve			$ xxx,xxx
Risk Based Costs			
Provision for Loan Losses			$ xxx,xxx
Capital Charges			$ xxx,xxx
Net Customer Profit Contribution			$ xxx,xxx
Sustaining Costs			
LOB Sustaining Costs	####	$ x.xxx	$ xxx,xxx
Channel Sustaining Costs	####	$ x.xxx	$ xxx,xxx
Market Sustaining Costs	####	$ x.xxx	$ xxx,xxx
Product Sustaining Costs	####	$ x.xxx	$ xxx,xxx
Enterprise Sustaining Costs	####	$ x.xxx	$ xxx,xxx
Brand Management	####	$ x.xxx	$ xxx,xxx
Regulatory Costs	####	$ x.xxx	$ xxx,xxx
Total Sustaining Costs			$ xxx,xxx
Total Costs			$ xxx,xxx
Economic Profit			$ xxx,xxx
Risk Adjusted Return on Capital			xx.xx%

ML ACCOUNT I CENTER I CUSTOMER I PRODUCT I BANKER

In short, you can dig deep and look at different aspects of your business with the power, focus, and clarity of an electron microscope—when everyone else has a cheap plastic magnifying glass like the kind you used in grade school.

SOLVING THE RUBIK'S CUBE

WHAT PROFITABILITY SYSTEMS DO...
Integration of Financial and Operational data into profitability analytics

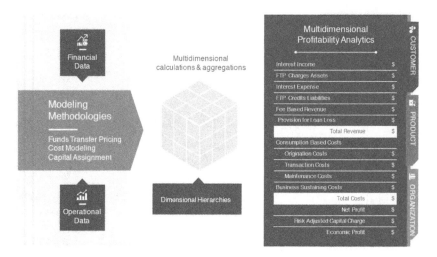

In profitability analytics, we're taking financial information from the general ledger—a wealth of operational data and statistics about what's going on in the business, what are the key drivers, what are the key volumes, what are the key measures, etc.—and then we're applying modeling methodologies to put them into a multidimensional cube of information that permits a common view across the different facets of the business.

The 3-D nature of profitability analytics contrasts with the flat, 2-D nature of general accounting. In the general ledger, there are only two basic dimensions you're working with: a GL account (such as salaries or benefits or occupancy) and an organizational unit (which business unit spent it.) That's very limiting.

In order to do multidimensional profitability analytics, we have to get down to the common element where all of the intersecting dimensions reside. In banking, for example, every individual account can tell you who the customer is, which products are associated with that account, what unit of the company it belongs to, etc. By capturing detailed financial and operational data at the customer account level detail, we can "roll it up" through these larger dimensional structures (product, unit, division, geography, etc.). Moreover, each of these dimension structures has associated hierarchies so that we can complement the analytics across what's really going on in the business, not just the two-dimensional financial structure.

By "roll up," I mean aggregating all the data points to paint the big picture. For example, you don't just want to see a giant list of customer accounts; you want to see the aggregated profitability of those accounts. Or say you have a common set of mortgage products; in the aggregate, all those products together form the company's mortgage business. And you can look at them at various points along the product hierarchy, from individual product, to product group, to product line, to macro level. In this way, you can navigate information about profitability across a range of crisscrossing dimensions. It gives you a much more nuanced understanding of the business' performance.

ARMADA DIMENSIONAL TREE - BANKING

Multidimensional profitability analytics starts at the customer account level

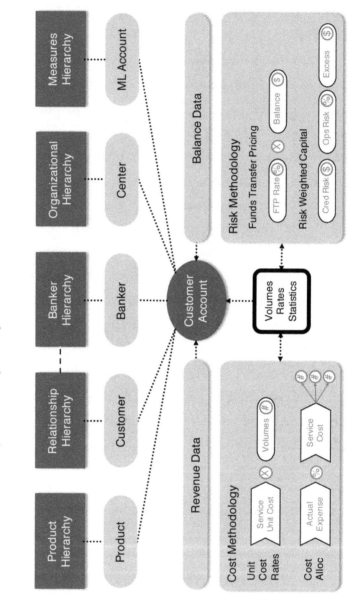

NAVIGATING HIERARCHIES

Once we have a "profitability fact table" at these intersecting dimensions, we can build hierarchies for each dimension and construct an "analytics cube" for users to navigate the data from a business intelligence application. For example, I could start at my particular center (or department) and see my overall profitability statement for my organization, then select or pivot the products dimension to see the same measures by the products I sell. I can further analyze those same measures by which customers contributed to my profitability. Hierarchies allow for the analysis across aggregation points (or roll-ups) of the detailed data. If I see an area of concern, I can drill into the underlying details all the way down the dimensional tree to the specific customer account and gain insights into what I can do differently to improve performance.

For most organizations, the customer account level represents the most "atomic" level of detail. Each customer account provides an understanding of the specific products and services they use; their specific salesperson or, in the case of banking, their assigned banker; what part of the organization or line of business they belong to; how marketing segments them demographically and geographically; and we understand how we have "booked" those financial measures in our general ledger systems. For revenues and balances, this is fairly easy as those details are interfaced into the general ledger system from our core operating systems (in banking, think loan and deposit systems).

And if you have thousands or millions of customer accounts, you want to see the bigger picture that they form. Maybe you want to look at commonalities or differences between customer accounts to detect patterns. For instance, you're the commercial banker assigned to two specific CEO customers. Joe and Bill are both long-time customers and run successful companies in your community. Both belong to a customer segment called "high-net-worth individuals" or "corporate relationships." Maybe Joe only leverages the commercial products of the bank and has no personal products, but Bill's banking relationship goes far beyond just the commercial products and his employees have hundreds of accounts at your bank. You can aggregate the profitability information of all customers affiliated with Bill's company. Now, you're starting to see the value of certain customer relationships at a much more granular level—starting at the lowest level of detail and aggregating it up through various defined hierarchies. You may price the next deal differently between these two customers, you may manage them differently, and you value their relationship to the bank very differently.

The point is that measuring profitability at this level of detail opens up a wide array of possibilities to segment customers across different dimensions to pinpoint certain profit-influencing behaviors and adjust your strategy accordingly.

Otherwise, in the absence of these capabilities, say you're only measuring profitability of accounts in your specific commercial or consumer business unit, or organization. A commercial banker in this situation may not see the differentiation between Joe and Bill, and may not be influenced by the additional business Bill brings to the consumer line of business, as it is not "in his lane," nor is he properly incented on this "book of business."

Other hierarchies can also play a role in profitability analytics. For example, I may want to know the profitability of commercial versus consumer divisions of a bank, but underneath those levels, I'd also want to know about the cost and profit of mortgage lending operations, or perhaps regional variations. There are various dimensional hierarchies that roll up along those lines. I need to drill down to the atomic level to be able to identify all these intersecting dimensions and then have hierarchies built above them to get a clear picture of the profitability "latticework" of the organization.

What makes profitability analytics so advantageous is that it allows us to measure disparate dimensions in the business using the *same profitability measures.* Whether you're looking at a checking account, or a mortgage loan, or a banking officer's performance, you're measuring them in a consistent manner. With each turn and click of the Rubik's Cube, your knowledge of the inner workings of the business grows.

Such an impressive depth, breadth, and detail of information is not just useful for upper-level management; it can also benefit banking officers, the sales team, and other frontline people, by giving them a multifaceted understanding of the profitability of their individual customers, so that they can better manage their customer base or price their products. At the end of the day, the platform enables you to measure and manage profitability across the key dimensions of your organization from one centralized source of actionable analytics.

SERVING THE RIGHT KIND OF CUSTOMER

Peter Drucker famously said that the purpose of a business is to create and serve a customer. That's only half-true—the point of business is to create and serve a *profitable* customer.

The typical accounting and finance reporting doesn't answer management questions: what lines of business to focus on to remain competitive, what businesses or product lines to exit, what product lines require a repricing or re-engineering. If we understand who are the most and least profitable customers, we can change our business to improve the performance of the organization as a whole.

Another important question involves how to better manage the primary levers of profitable growth, which in banks means risks, margins, and costs. Early in my career, before I became an entrepreneur, I was working in the finance department of large commercial bank. The sales group was working on a major deal with a prospective customer—a national retailer that wanted us to handle the entirety of its cash management business. It was such a big client, with such complex analytical demands, that bringing them on would require us to buy entirely new equipment—but the accompanying revenue boost would make these cost outlays worthwhile. On this basis, we assumed it was a good deal.

Eventually, we persuaded them to sign on, gave some excessive discounts, and as expected, their business brought a healthy revenue boost.

But all that glitters is not gold. Once we implemented profitability analytics and aligned all of the costs associated with the additional services that we were providing that particular customer, it turned out that despite the increase in revenue, serving the new client actually incurred a net loss. We had been so focused on top-line revenue that we were sure the client would be profitable, but our analysis proved otherwise.

In order to thrive in business, you have to be able to turn setbacks into opportunities for growth and change. We had miscalculated our bet and were losing money on what we thought was an excellent deal, but we couldn't simply cut the new customer loose, and we had already paid for the infrastructure upgrades to increase our capacity to serve them. It was evident that we would have to leverage our expanded capacity to bring on *additional* customers to make the investment a profitable one.

So instead of just focusing on how we could serve this one customer, we really should have been looking at how to expand that line of business to fully utilize the extra infrastructure costs.

This is a telling example of how the capability to look at customer and product profitability on its own leads you to a better understanding of the economics of your business, not just the accounting income and expenses and net income. You can really start to understand what levers you can pull to increase the profitability of the organization.

One thing I've learned over several decades in this field is that size doesn't matter. We serve some of the most prominent financial services companies in the world, but a twenty-billion-dollar bank can be just as profitable as a fifty-billion-dollar bank even though one looks bigger than the other. Profitability analytics lets you perform better than bigger and more complex competitors, even if your revenue is lower.

ACTIONABLE INSIGHTS
Charts from the battlefields

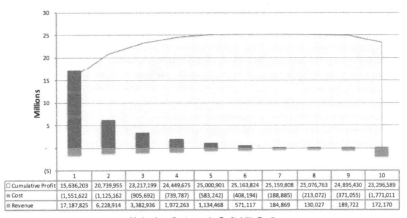

	1	2	3	4	5	6	7	8	9	10
☐ Cumulative Profit	15,636,203	20,739,955	23,217,199	24,449,675	25,000,901	25,163,824	25,159,808	25,076,763	24,895,430	23,296,589
▦ Cost	(1,551,622)	(1,125,162)	(905,692)	(739,787)	(583,242)	(408,194)	(188,885)	(213,072)	(371,055)	(1,771,011)
▦ Revenue	17,187,825	6,228,914	3,382,936	1,972,263	1,134,468	571,117	184,869	130,027	189,722	172,170

Market Area Customers by Profitability Decline
☐ Cumulative Profit ▪ Revenue ▦ Cost

The above chart is from an actual profitability analytics project we did. Profitability is divided into deciles, starting with the top 10 percent of the customer base followed by the next 10 percent most profitable, and so on, all the way down the line. This is a common type of reporting in profitability analytics and it isn't just limited to customers. We can represent the profitability of all the different dimensions, for example, the most to the least profitable products, geographies, or divisions.

In this chart, the curve arcing across the top is known as a whale curve and shows you the cumulative profitability of the organization as you aggregate the deciles, from most to least profitable. It shows the Pareto principle (aka the 80/20 rule) in effect. In this case, the top 20 percent of customers comprise around 80 percent of the company's profitability. After that, there's quite a steep drop-off.

That's a staggering figure, but I've seen this phenomenon manifested in even more extreme ways. In one organization I assisted, the top 25 percent of customers made up 200 percent of their total profit while all the other customers basically caused losses, equaling 100 percent of their total profit. Imagine what an impact it would have on their business if they cut the loss-making clients and kept the money-making ones.

You'd think such dramatic imbalances would be glaringly obvious to the executive team, but they're not. Profitability analytics shines a light into the dark corners where accounting can't reach, allowing leaders to make better decisions about which areas of business are generating value and which are dead weight.

DIMENSIONAL HIERARCHIES

Product Hierarchy

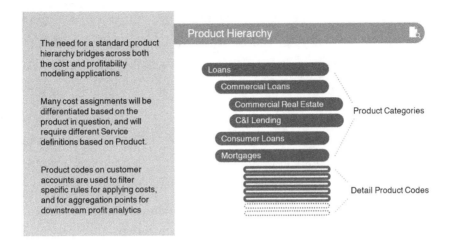

The need for a standard product hierarchy bridges across both the cost and profitability modeling applications.

Many cost assignments will be differentiated based on the product in question, and will require different Service definitions based on Product.

Product codes on customer accounts are used to filter specific rules for applying costs, and for aggregation points for downstream profit analytics

Product Hierarchy

Loans
Commercial Loans
Commercial Real Estate
C&I Lending
Consumer Loans
Mortgages

Product Categories

Detail Product Codes

DIMENSIONAL HIERARCHIES

Hierarchies and Attributes

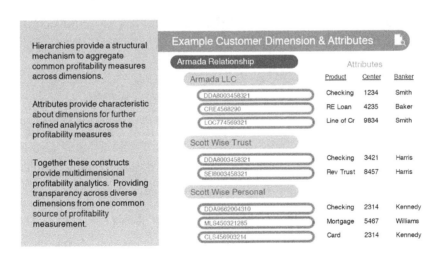

Hierarchies provide a structural mechanism to aggregate common profitability measures across dimensions.

Attributes provide characteristic about dimensions for further refined analytics across the profitability measures

Together these constructs provide multidimensional profitability analytics. Providing transparency across diverse dimensions from one common source of profitability measurement.

Example Customer Dimension & Attributes

Armada Relationship

	Attributes		
Armada LLC	Product	Center	Banker
DDA8003458321	Checking	1234	Smith
CRE4568290	RE Loan	4235	Baker
LOC774569321	Line of Cr	9834	Smith
Scott Wise Trust			
DDA8003458321	Checking	3421	Harris
SEI8003458321	Rev Trust	8457	Harris
Scott Wise Personal			
DDA9662004310	Checking	2314	Kennedy
MLS450321285	Mortgage	5467	Williams
CLS456903214	Card	2314	Kennedy

THE SATISFACTION OF BEING PLEASANTLY SURPRISED

People want to do the right thing and they want to build a good business. When they get the information that empowers them to do so, it energizes and excites them. It's satisfying to us from a consulting perspective to see them apply that in actionable, on-the-ground ways.

I always enjoy our "big reveal meetings" with new clients, when they're first able to look at their own company's data through a multi-dimensional-profitability lens. Until that moment, they've never had the capacity to research customer items on demand. Instead, if executives had a specific question about some highly detailed concern, they'd send an analyst to wade through multiple data systems to research the answer.

Clients are often skeptical when arriving at these meetings, since they've never had such a powerful analytic tool at their fingertips. It's like the executives have been roaming a parched desert for days, and by the time I offer them water, they're not sure if their eyes are deceiving them. They look at it up close, smell it, maybe swish it around into the glass to examine what it is they are about to drink. They just can't believe it's real.

One company I've worked with recently comes to mind. While unveiling a presentation to their management committee, which included the chairman of their board, their president, the chief operating officer, the chief financial officer, and the chief risk officer, I showed them a series of graphics similar to the one we saw earlier in this chapter: their most profitable customers, their most profitable bankers, their most successful lines of business, their top products, etc.

At first, they weren't moved. These are people who are luminaries in their field, who are not easily swayed by "eye candy charts," and they're used to salesmen trying to impress them with technical jargon and elaborate graphs. But as we continued through the presentation, and were able to really demonstrate what profitability analytics is about and what it does—that it's ultimately not just a jumble of numbers and terms and abstract math, but directly connected to real, impactful, strategic business decisions—the executives in the room perked up.

One executive had been putting together a deal with a customer, and this deal was giving him some concern because of its risks. So he wanted to know, "Are we making enough money to justify the risk with this customer?" In other words, when he looked at the analytics for this specific customer, would he see that the revenue received was greater than the cost of funding, cost of capital, and the cost to serve this client in order to generate a profit?

Lesser consultants might deflect such a question, or respond with the familiar, unsatisfying, "I'll get back to you later with an answer," but we said, "Sure, give me the name of the customer and we'll search right now for it." I pull up the customer account, we examine the measures, and give him the answers to his questions, right then and there.

So, he drank that water down to the last drop. Now every executive wanted a drink too, and in unison they all started rattling off account numbers and customer names they wanted to examine. Already, they were buying in.

When they have credibility in the information, they're seeing the analytics at work, they're able to question the methods behind it, and they're satisfied that finally there is one version of the truth in terms of profitability and cost, then their minds immediately shift to "How can I leverage this throughout my enterprise to drive better performance?" It's great to see that at work.

In the next chapter, we'll look at strategic cost modeling, which enhances understanding of the economics of a business by revealing the causal drivers of expenses incurred across the enterprise.

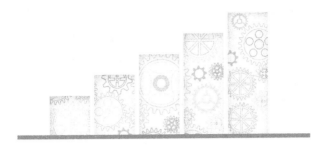

CHAPTER SIX
THE INS AND OUTS OF STRATEGIC COST MODELING

Executives cannot understand the economics of their business without credible, transparent cost information. But getting the right kind of information can be challenging. Conventional cost management applications are methodologically rigid and inflexible. Fortunately, there are better, faster, and more cutting-edge ways to understand the drivers of cost in large, complex organizations.

Strategic cost modeling (SCM) involves taking the occurrence of expenses as recorded in accounting and modeling them into specific cost components that describe the business purpose, activity, or service that *caused* the expense as a result of consumer activity. It provides transparency into the underlying economics of the business and the causal drivers of expense incurred across the enterprise, and it allows you to rapidly identify inefficiencies, unnecessary spending, and opportunities for cost takeout, among other applications.

Any given activity performed during the course of business has costs. In some cases, the costs are easily quantifiable. But what is the true cost of acquiring a new customer? Or processing a teller transaction? Often, for the vast number of consumer-facing activities undertaken by a business, there are ancillary costs that aren't captured by GAAP expense reporting and must be revealed with the microscopic vision of a different analytic method.

For example, you're running a bank and you want to understand the costs involved in new loan origination. For every new loan, a panoply of functions—personal, technological, infrastructural, fiscal—are required to carry it out. Originating the loan requires employees to handle it. It requires technology to process it. It requires facilities (lights, furniture, a roof over your head) to make the whole process possible.

That's just for one loan. But you're processing many loans every month. And that number is not static. If there's a sudden surge in demand for loans, with more and more customers borrowing money, there could be a concomitant spike in costs. You'll need more credit underwriters, which means you're going to spend more money on salaries in that department. Tracking all of these fluctuating, multifaceted expenses can get very complex. But SCM models all of it, down to the finest detail.

Strategic cost modeling is an analytics-focused management framework designed to provide transparency into the underlying economics of a business and the causal drivers of expenses incurred across the enterprise.

The main components of an SCM program include:

- understanding patterns of consumption of products and services across the enterprise and demand placed on company resources,

- modeling of unit cost information to identify causal drivers of expense in the delivery of products and services,

- developing a cost-recovery ecosystem to manage demand on shared services functions to promote a partnership of cost management between front and back office,

- and providing advanced cost analytics to support fact-based cost improvement decisions and establish enterprise cost controls.

With SCM, we can create models of unit cost information that really connect those drivers of expense from product/service delivery back into the accounting. From there, we can start to be more forward-looking and can leverage the information to make real, actionable changes to how we do business. The model provides better, fact-based information for cost improvements and cost controls, just like in the earlier story about the bank executives who were contemplating outsourcing, but who were limited in their outlook since they only had a blunt, two-dimensional view of expenses. Once we added strategic cost modeling to the mix, they could suddenly see the myriad "layers" and how the services provided in different units of the company were impacting expenses from an accounting perspective.

Better vision leads to better decisions. That's strategic cost modeling defined.

FOLLOWING THE RIGHT PATH: CUSTOMER TO ORGANIZATION

The diagram below shows what a cost model looks like conceptually. It underscores the fact that we understand revenue according to customer, but expenses we only know by organization. *The key premise of cost modeling is to identify a traceable, causal relationship between the customer choices and economic benefit. It begins with the demand placed on the organization by a customer, not with what an organization incurs in expenses.*

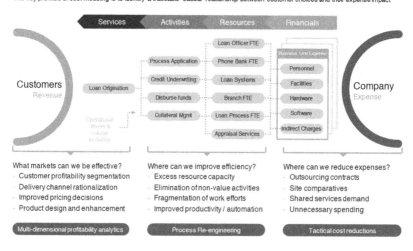

Not beginning with the end in mind is one of the biggest causes of modeling failure. Instead of starting with the expenses and then allocating them to other things, you must first examine the source demand or the source service that's being consumed. Then, you can ask yourself the key questions undergirding creation of the model: Where can we reduce expenses? Where can we improve efficiency? And in what markets can we be effective?

Every dollar of expense should be an investment seeking a return. That's fundamental. If you're figuring out what is driving expenses, start by examining customer behaviors. Examples of drivers could be account overdraft, or customers who interface with a teller versus using the ATM, or the act of opening a new account. Those are the consumer drivers that cause a company to spend money, so that's where the model should start.

Now, you can ask, "What work activities have to be performed to deliver those services?" It could be credit underwriting, collecting data about the customer, making decisions around risk, or fulfilling the loan, among other tasks. You must also determine what resources are needed to perform those activities, and where on the financials are the expenses for those resources recorded.

From all of that, you can create operational drivers and statistics between all four of the dimensions in the figure—services, activities, resources, and financials—and connect the model of the expenses to the revenue. Then they become *costs per product/service.* Now you can trace that all the way back through the different links in the chain: a given product costs X in salary expense in this department, Y dollars in occupancy or facilities expense, Z in software expense, so on and so on.

Great, but where do you go next? Well, once that model is completed, you can start to answer the tough questions involved in multidimensional profitability. For example, in the left-third of the diagram, which represents the "customers" side of the equation, we can begin to understand what markets we can operate effectively in since now we can perform customer profitability segmentation based on specific services used and the volume consumed by each customer. We can do delivery channel rationalization of customer profitability, based on whether they deposit that check from their iPhone, an ATM, or a branch teller. We can improve pricing decisions and redesign products to optimize profitability based on how a customer uses (or abuses) our services, now that we have a more complete understanding of costs.

The middle third of the model is more concerned with process re-engineering and directs our focus to how we can improve efficiency. For example, it might tell us where we have excess capacity. If we have fifty credit underwriters in a single department and half of them have nothing to do all day because mortgage loan originations are declining, then we need to remove some of that excess capacity to be more profitable. The model tells us, accurately and precisely, that it might be time to let some of those people go, or at least redeploy those personnel resources to a strategic-growth area of the business.

Another benefit of the process re-engineering stage of SCM is reduction of labor fragmentation. If I have twenty credit underwriters, all of whom spend five percent of their time doing some administrative work, it would be better to have one administrator handle all of the administrative stuff, freeing up the underwriters to spend more time on more profitable, high-skilled, specialized tasks.

Or we can find actionable solutions to improve productivity and automation. Nowadays, there's not any physical credit underwriting for an auto loan or a credit card or other commodity-type financial services because they've been largely automated.

Or maybe we need to eliminate non-value added activities that incur costs but don't increase profit, such as the aforementioned example of the inefficient exception processes afflicting the bank that was contemplating an outsourcing. Or additionally quantify the costs of regulatory activities to support lobbyists in government. The middle part of that model gives the ability to do all of these things.

Finally, the back segment of the model—tactical cost reductions— deals more with expenses. How can we reduce them? How can we do the same things we do now, but do them less expensively? Should we outsource certain functions? Are we using our internal resources effectively? Can we cut superfluous expenses like the corporate jet?

In this way, effective cost modeling draws a clear roadmap between customers (revenue) and organization (expenses) and provides vital information to let you make actionable changes at every step of the way.

THE EVOLUTION OF COST TRANSPARENCY

In life, love, and strategic cost modeling, the more you give, the more you get. Getting started might be slow going (and most companies never get very far), but once you start building an effective modeling program, progress advances exponentially rather than linearly. The benefits begin to accrue quickly. An incremental investment of time and effort yields better information, which in turn drives better, more strategic actions.

EVOLUTION OF COST TRANSPARENCY

Companies continue to evolve cost analytics to drive strategic value

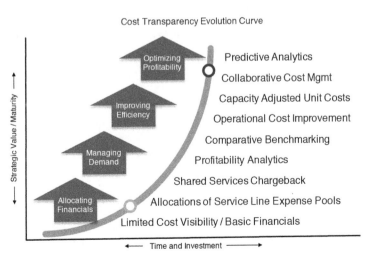

Cost Transparency Evolution Curve

The above figure depicts what I call the "evolution of cost transparency." Most organizations operate at the bottom of that curve. They have limited cost visibility because they're looking at their basic financials or the basic accounting. The ones who mature are able to do some level of allocations of service line expense pools, but then they start to advance their use of cost information very quickly once they've built these models. They can get into shared services chargeback, where IT or HR can charge the other departments for costs incurred. Then, above that, they can start doing profitability analytics, which we talked about in the previous chapter.

Firms that advance beyond that step can do comparative benchmarking against their cost of performance of certain services versus comparable services. They can look at doing cost takeout and operational cost improvement. Still, more advanced models can start to really measure the cost of excess capacity, especially around labor, which is a big thing these days.

Higher up the curve, when you really get everybody working together across departments, you can achieve collaborative cost management and have the whole organization working in sync instead of in departmental silos. Beyond that, the ultimate goal, the holy grail of all of these analytics, is to have predictive analytics, where you can accurately forecast expenses based on forecasted volumes of growth by products and services.

Having transparency into underlying profitability measures across all dimensions allows the users to "self-serve" their questions regarding what makes up the components of specific costs or other financial measures in the resulting profitability analytics. This is a big deal for companies with lean finance teams supporting the analytics. Without transparent information, cost and profitability systems become this impenetrable "black box" of underlying methodologies and data elements, and business users are constantly requesting the finance team to explain, analyze, and defend the numbers.

Exposing the elements in a transparent analytics user environment empowers the business to conduct specific analysis that informs the practical decisions they are trying to make.

For example, if a user is trying to make a marginal pricing decision for a customer, they might see a unit cost for a particular service as $150 per unit, but to make the deal competitive, they may need to price under $130 per unit. If they have the transparency into the underlying components of that unit cost, they may find that $40 per unit of that cost is associated with fixed costs (e.g., costs related to the building that houses their office). These costs are going to be incurred whether or not they make that individual deal. If they have that *transparency*, they can confidently reduce the price because the marginal or incremental cost to of the deal is below the price they want to offer to win the business.

REALIZING VALUE FROM AN INVESTMENT IN COST ANALYTICS

The three primary levers for sustainable cost optimization and control

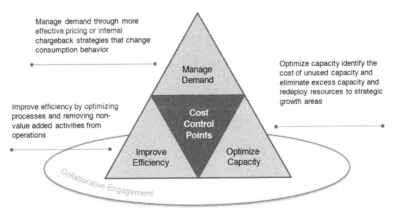

The goal is to create one consistent source of credible unit cost data that engages the business with information to drive profitable business outcomes.

Ultimately, to practically apply the information gleaned from cost analytics, there are only three levers you can pull. You can manage demand and moderate consumption of services via more effective pricing or an internal chargeback strategy. For example, if your bank charged you two dollars every time you went to the teller but the direct or mobile deposit was free, that would be an effort to moderate demand by encouraging customers to use the alternate channels (which incur lower costs for the bank).

The second lever you can pull is improving efficiency by optimizing processes, removing exceptions and non-value added activities, and generally getting faster and better in product and service delivery.

Finally, you can optimize capacity, which means making sure your labor capacity matches demand and try to create as much variable cost structure as possible, so that you don't have too much or too little capacity for performing work. SCM is very good at identifying the labor capacity and provides guidance on how to surgically redeploy personnel resources to strategic growth areas. That could entail layoffs, or shifting around your people to where they can best serve the organization.

However you apply it, credible cost data drives profitable business outcomes.

TACTICAL VERSUS STRATEGIC COST MODELING

We call it *strategic* cost modeling for a reason. SCM, which is more focused on high-level probability information, is related to, but distinct from, *activity-based costing* (ABC), which is more tactical in nature. *Activity-based costing* (ABC) or operational cost analytics require much more detailed data than SCM. It focuses more on the activities and processes and on what work is being performed, not necessarily the more strategic driver of what is the customer consuming. What I call strategic cost modeling is an adaption of ABC, but SCM takes it to the next level in terms of what you can do with the information, in the context of actionable profitability analytics.

Basically, ABC is a cost accounting technique that seeks to line up costs to different overhead activities and assign costs to the products and services produced by the company. One distinction between ABC and SCM is that ABC starts with the expense and then tries to allocate it. It's more of an accounting exercise. It is useful for certain functions, but at heart, it doesn't really expand one's understanding of the business economics because it rarely starts with the causal *driver* of expense, which is customer behavior—some demand that the customer has placed on the organization that causes those costs to happen.

The limitation of ABC is that if you go in and start asking different departments how they spend the expenses they manage, you get way into the weeds and disconnected from what you really want to look at strategically: what is the customer doing to cause these expenses?

Let's revisit the cost model design diagram below, which calls attention to the distinction between a high-level strategic approach (which requires less granular data) and a more operational, tactical view (which demands more granular data). Like Goldilocks and the three bears, the art of cost-modeling seeks a "just right" balance: the optimal midpoint between the cost of errors (inadequate measurement) versus the cost of measurement (too much or too detailed measurement).

Say you are figuring out which activities cost what for whom in a business. If you're aiming to allocate costs, and an employee gives you a list of one hundred different things that they do in the course of a day, a lot of those aren't really going to have any material impact on *the cost of a service,* so that information isn't useful. Why go through the effort of trying to measure inconsequential data that doesn't drive strategic decisions?

I'm reminded of a story from early in my career that showed how an overabundance of data becomes counterproductive. To measure the workday habits of bank employees, we would conduct a kind of time motion study using fancy bar code readers called TimeWands. We would have the tellers go through a list of activities one by one, as they performed them, during a two-week study period. They would scan the barcode when they started and they would scan the barcode when they finished, measuring the time it took to perform each activity.

After, we would take the data back to the manager of that particular area or department and say, "I've seen that this activity takes anywhere from thirty-five seconds to four minutes. Here's the array of times recorded by the tellers during the study period." Then the managers would go, "Well, let's just pick two minutes," and that would become the benchmark.

And on it went, for every little process performed by a worker in the course of a workday, using TimeWands to capture that granular level of measurement only for someone else to say, "Well, it looks like an average of two minutes."

The exercise was giving us a wealth of information at the operational level, but it wasn't a very *strategic* approach. What were all these minutiae supposed to tell us about how to steer the company?

Sure, doing it that way wouldn't provide as *accurate* a measurement of employee time usage. But for the strategic purpose at hand, it was adequate. The tedious, blow-by-blow, down-to-the-finest-detail record-taking we were doing with TimeWands was data excess—it wasn't providing the meaningful strategic information value. At the end of the long hike up, the view wasn't worth the climb.

Of course, there might be situations where that granularity of information might serve a legitimate business purpose. But what we're trying to do with SCM is more "high-level"—strategic customer-focused, rather than operational. With SCM, we want to create models that drive big-picture decisions. And we don't need to track the start and end times of a hundred tasks for a small business unit to do that.

Less is more.

Unfortunately, this truth eludes eager managers who equate "accuracy" with "credibility" when it comes to data collection. I have to explain to them that the cost of providing and sustaining that type of modeling is not worth the benefits that it generates. *The information is only as valuable as the action it initiates—actionable* analytics, after all.

The obvious question, of course, is, "Well then, how do you strike the right balance?" And there is no easy answer to that, except to take each challenge as it comes and do the hard work of figuring out the "just right" point. It really is an art. It takes a lot of effort and a lot of skill (and the right technology to facilitate the process.) But when done correctly, it can revolutionize your business.

FROM "ON PAPER TO "IN PRACTICE": MOVING FROM METHODOLOGY TO IMPLEMENTATION

Costs are the most controllable part of the profit equation, and business leaders face ceaseless pressure to keep them down. However, there are only so many ways to cut costs before it starts to adversely affect the organization.

SCM has opened up a new front in the perennial battle to minimize costs and offer a sustainable approach to measuring business economics. Advances in methodology and technology have brought a resurgence in cost modeling as a foundational element of an enterprise cost management program that integrates finance, planning, and analytics. The tactical outlook of ABC combines with the strategic focus of cost modeling to provide a powerful analytical tool that drives savvy, forward-thinking business decisions.

In Section II of this book, we examined the role of guiding principles, which provide a foundation, define the mission, and create the rules of the road that keep an analytics program (and its stakeholders) on track. We examined multidimensional profitability analytics, which, like a Rubik's Cube, untangles the complex intersection of crisscrossing elements of an organization in a way that gives you a three-dimensional look at where your business generates the most (and least) profit. And we studied how strategic cost modeling, which starts with consumer behavior and "works backwards" to create transparency into the firm's underlying economics, enabling the organization to better manage demand, improve efficiency, and optimize capacity.

Thus far, our focus has mostly been on the value of these analytics and the methodologies required—setting the stage for execution. The real challenge of *implementation* awaits us. That's the topic of Section III. In Chapter 7, we'll talk about design (how information is modeled) and architecture (systems and data requirements needed for the solution). Chapter 8 addresses how to assess your capabilities as you get ready for implementation. In Chapter 9, we'll wade into deployment strategies and examine how to navigate change. Then, Chapter 10 will take a final look at what we've covered, and also look ahead—to how profitability and cost analytics can transform *your* organization.

SECTION III

THINK BIG, START SMALL, AND DELIVER INCREMENTAL VALUE: IMPLEMENTATION

CHAPTER SEVEN
DESIGN AND ARCHITECTURE

Before we get into design and architecture, let's talk generally about implementation, the subject of this section. Implementation is not a single moment but an ongoing process that must be iterated as it unfolds—a journey, rather than a destination.

It's a lot more than just flipping a switch and watching the analytics program flicker to life. You need to be actively engaged in the project to sustain it, fixing problems as they emerge and making improvements as you track the system's performance. It's constantly evolving with every iteration.

That journey consists of three cyclical phases: 1) measuring and modeling; 2) analyzing and acting; and 3) predicting and planning. Most organizations never evolve beyond Phase 1. They spend all their time trying to get the perfect modeling methodology but they fail to act on it, which inhibits them from accelerating *benefit realization*: "in-flight" performance and profitability analysis that delivers value early. Good implementations are on time and on budget; great implementations are self-funding by providing tangible benefits whose financial value exceeds their implementation costs.

Even fewer organizations reach the "predict and plan" stage, which gives them forward-looking analytic capacity and allows for accelerated *strategic integration* throughout the enterprise. Strategic integration means synergistic connections with finance, or other high-profile strategic programs that can leverage the newly acquired information. We can integrate with product pricing types of decisions, planning, or even conduct some predictive analysis around customer lifetime value. The more areas in which we can leverage the profitability information, the stronger the strategic integration will be.

Of course, that is contingent on creating *sustainable processes* that allow the team to update and manage production cycles on an iterative release schedule, so that the team can spend less time generating information and more time gaining actionable insights. And the client can maintain it within their own resource constraints long after we're gone.

The underlying point throughout the whole cycle is that we must strive to provide analytics that drive profitable business behaviors without letting the pursuit of perfection inhibit us from attaining actionable results—from information, to insight, to impact.

As demonstrated in the following figure, a successful profitability analytics program should start with a solid foundation in methodology, data, and governance—all the things we talked about at length in Section II. A house built on a weak foundation will not stand. Similarly, the better the analytics foundation is, the longer it can be leveraged throughout the organization.

PROFITABILITY PROGRAM
Establishing an iterative development approach for speed to value

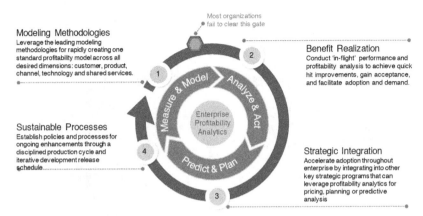

Modeling Methodologies
Leverage the leading modeling methodologies for rapidly creating one standard profitability model across all desired dimensions: customer, product, channel, technology and shared services.

Most organizations fail to clear this gate

Benefit Realization
Conduct 'in-flight' performance and profitability analysis to achieve quick hit improvements, gain acceptance, and facilitate adoption and demand.

Sustainable Processes
Establish policies and processes for ongoing enhancements through a disciplined production cycle and iterative development release schedule.

Strategic Integration
Accelerate adoption throughout enterprise by integrating into other key strategic programs that can leverage profitability analytics for pricing, planning or predictive analysis

Enterprise Profitability Analytics

Measure & Model · Analyze & Act · Predict & Plan

Every iteration is focused on providing analytics that drive profitable business behaviors, not letting the 'pursuit of perfection' delay the 'achievement of improvement'

On top of that, you begin adding the "advanced modeling analytics" that define your measurement methodologies and the calculations to be performed. From that point, the focus becomes driving value from the analytics, through deployment, to the user community, and begin to integrate it into other predictive modeling functions, climbing higher and higher until you're able to achieve enterprise adoption—fully integrating the analytics into the day-to-day operations that drive more profitable business decisions.

Each of these layers of the pyramid involves its own "sub-process"—what I call the "four Ds": discover, design, develop, and deploy.

ARMADA'S COST & PROFITABILITY ANALYTICS FRAMEWORK

Proven framework to establish a solid foundation for profitability analytics

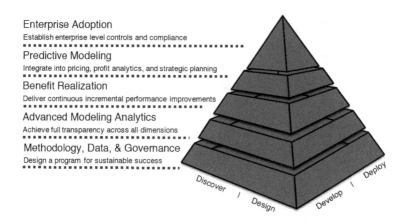

Enterprise Adoption
Establish enterprise level controls and compliance

Predictive Modeling
Integrate into pricing, profit analytics, and strategic planning

Benefit Realization
Deliver continuous incremental performance improvements

Advanced Modeling Analytics
Achieve full transparency across all dimensions

Methodology, Data, & Governance
Design a program for sustainable success

Discover / Design / Develop / Deploy

Prior to deployment, we always assess the client's capabilities compared to leading practices—the gap analysis, which I'll discuss more in the following chapter. Then we deliver an assessment that describes the lay of the land and what is possible within the organization's unique capabilities and their current resource capacity. From there, we go into design, where we create solution blueprints, make recommendations, and create a delivery roadmap. That puts us in a position to execute the prototype, or proof of value, that confirms the design, methodologies, and analytics capabilities desired by the organization.

This leads into the development phase, where we find ways to mitigate project risk and draw on our library of implementation accelerators. Often, it is challenging for clients to start from scratch on any aspect of the project. Implementation accelerators are tools and templates of leading practices we have created to jumpstart their process.[2]

---

2   The benefit of working with a firm as niche and experienced as ours is that our toolbelt is filled with implementation accelerators from many projects of the

Finally, there is deployment, the phase in which we're really looking for user acceptance and refinement, generating opportunity analysis, training and change management, and sustainability planning for ongoing production.

Note that the "four Ds" framework applies to *each* phase of the implementation (methodology, data, and governance; advanced cost analytics, benefit realization, predictive modeling, and enterprise adoption). Armada's implementation framework is a many-layered, multi-tiered engine made up of a process within a process within a process. Like an engine in a car, it's a lot of pistons and valves and connecting rods moving and clanking together. And it evolves as the analytics system grows. It might be staggeringly complex, but this methodical approach is what holds everything together and keeps the parts moving in sync. This approach has served our clients well, delivering on time and on budget and promising a clear understanding of what is involved in every phase of the program. The framework mitigates delivery risk and helps our clients avoid the common pitfalls encountered by many other organizations.

THE FIVE PITFALLS

There are five common pitfalls that I've observed during my three decades developing and implementing actionable analytics in large organizations.

---

past. For example, if the client needs to define activities for their cost model design, we have an activity dictionary for common activities at similar organizations. Armada has many project accelerators and templates, such as a volume capture process and template on how to engage and communicate with data services to get what you need, and a host of other tools.

FIVE MOST COMMON PROJECT PITFALLS
Programs can be complex with many risks to mitigate

Issue	Implication	Risk Mitigation
Technology Centric Focus Technology selection precedes program methodology design and definition	! Program focuses on technology implementation instead of business outcome ! Technology platform becomes constraining factor in successful program – constant rework	Methodology design should drive technology deployment with defined stakeholder engagement and credible data sources
Implementation Execution An over ambitious implementation or inadequate strategy without committed and capable resources	! Missed project timelines, budget overruns ! Diminished credibility with business ! Unrealized expectations and benefit	Detailed assessment of internal capabilities and gap analysis with a comprehensive roadmap that delivers incremental value
Design and Governance Program fails to take a consistent enterprise approach and establish target business use and governance strategy	! Program viewed as Finance only system ! Lack of business buy-in and stakeholder support ! Failed adoption across company	Early establishment of program rules of engagement, stakeholder governance, and leadership that can drive transformational change
Sustainable Processes Design and implementation strategies are over-engineered without considering resource capacity or capability to maintain	! Finance team becomes dedicated to maintaining system instead of driving business value from analytics ! Data becomes stale and unusable	Dedicated resourcing of program with capabilities that will continuously drive business value to the enterprise and own the ongoing systems and processes
Data Management Underestimated requirements for sourcing data and resolving data quality issues	! Diminished credibility in information ! Wasted resources waiting on perfect data ! Incomplete system rollout	Comprehensive understanding of common data sources and strategies to manage SCM data quality

Technology-centric focus

We've all seen this one before—the tech-happy exec who just returned from a big convention, convinced that the flashy piece of software he saw demoed is going to be the silver bullet that solves the company's problems.

It's a tempting prospect (who wouldn't want a quick fix?), but it doesn't work that way. Technology is just a means to an end, not the end itself. It's a tool, and it's only as good as the person handling it. You can put a hammer in the hands of a five-year-old, or in the hands of a skilled carpenter, and you're going to get radically different results.

Technology is important, but it shouldn't be the starting point. Otherwise, you could end up stuck with the wrong software infra-structure, and find yourself trying to fit a round peg into a square hole. Instead, begin by formulating your desired business outcomes, and plan your technological needs around that.

Overambitious execution

This is a common pitfall in corporate projects in general, not just in the profitability analytics field. But because of the complexity of profitability analytics, the risk here is even higher. Unrealistic expectations, missed deadlines, cost overruns—they can all add up quickly to botch the implementation.

You need to think of execution as a process, rather than a single point in time—it's a journey, not a destination. I know you might be tired of that phrase by now, but it's one of the central concepts of Section III, and really, a theme underlying the entire subject of actionable analytics. The program is continually evolving over time, which requires continuous improvement and refinement at the margins.

One of the key ways that we mitigate the risk of this pitfall is to conduct a thorough, upfront assessment of an enterprise's internal capabilities and perform a gap analysis addressing what needs to be achieved to get from the current state to the target state.

Lack of design governance upfront

Usually this occurs because of a lack of buy-in among stakeholders. Profitability analytics is not just a "finance project." It's a strategic program for the organization as a whole, and so the whole organization must be committed to it. The goals must be clear; the guiding principles must be universally accepted; and the various stakeholders must understand their role and play their part. And of course, you need dedicated leaders to see the whole thing through and make sure everyone in the boat is rowing in the same direction.

To mitigate the risk of inadequate design governance, secure buy-in and establish governance protocols at the beginning. It should be "ready, aim, fire," not "fire, ready, aim."

Lack of sustainability

You've got the analytics program up and running—now what? You need to keep it rolling once it "goes live," and continue its operation long after the consultants have gone home. Too often, people get caught up in finding the most technically elegant solution or the most accurate methodology, and, in the process, lose sight of the fact that they're going to need twenty people to maintain the analytics system each month. That's going to be pretty hard when you have a staff of five.

You've got to think ahead, beyond the planning, beyond the launch, to make sure you have the brainpower and resources to maintain an analytics program long-term. Don't leap before you look. Proper design, stable architecture, and efficient production processes are the main way to avoid this pitfall.

Bad data management

Data is the wellspring of analytics. Without quality data coming in, in a timely manner, the well dries up. Bad data going in yields bad analytics coming out.

Most organizations dramatically underestimate the quantity and quality of the data that's required for actionable analytics. Or they commit the opposite error of having *too* much data, causing them to waste resources (such as personnel, or software expenses) in a costly pursuit of "perfect" data far beyond what the system needs to function. This is sometimes described as the "measurement versus errors" tradeoff, which we've talked about a few times already. You need to find that sweet spot between cost and accuracy. This pitfall can also be mitigated through proper design and architecture, which is the focus of the rest of the chapter.

BUILT TO LAST: DESIGN AND ARCHITECTURE

Put simply, *design and architecture are the solution plan to execute the profitability methodologies in a repeatable system of analytics and reporting.* If governance and guiding principles are the foundation, design and architecture are the blueprints. But a good architect doesn't just put lines on the paper when building a house. He thinks about the intended use, vision, and style of what the occupant is going to do with the property. Design is all about taking the methodology you have defined and bringing it to life with the details of dimensions, structures, modeling, data, processes, and technology, defining how these elements come together to produce the desired outcomes.

The image below shows the different components—and as you can see, there are many—of a profitability analytics architecture. Each of those grey boxes (contributors, unit cost modeling, user community, etc.) represent a piece of the whole. Put together, they comprise the entire design—a whole that is greater than the sum of its parts.

SOLUTION ARCHITECTURE
Functional Overview

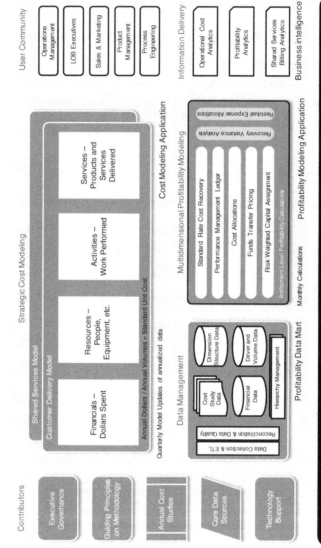

But before we look at the big picture, let's break it down into bite-sized pieces, in keeping with the theme of this section of *thinking big, starting small, and delivering incremental value.*

We always want to begin with the end in mind, so we start off with the user community, who are both the contributors to the design and the beneficiaries of the solution. In this step, we decide who comprises the stakeholder steering committee or governance board that makes important decisions about the protocol, scope, and rules of engagement for the profitability analytics program.

This user community defines all the functionality that we need to build out in the implementation phase. They can include people from operations management, business executives, marketing and product management, finance and accounting people, and even process engineering. Together, they make up a cross-functional group of stakeholders who can fine-tune the design criteria to fit the project's objectives.

Reporting and analytics (which can include operational cost reporting, organizational profitability, and customer profitability) is another piece of the whole. One of the key areas of implementation involves defining and reporting the target sets of analytics that we want to create, depending on the business goals. They might be operational in nature if we want to use the analytics to improve efficiency. They might involve managing performance and paying incentives among employees, or they might consider how to deliver valuable information to the customer-service people so they understand the profitability of certain clients. Whatever the case, it's necessary to define upfront what type of information we want to deliver to the right people in order to encourage more profitable behaviors.

Also relevant to reporting and analytics is the choice of technology—what sort of BI (business intelligence) platform will be utilized.

ACTIONABLE PROFITABILITY ANALYTICS

There are many flavors of visualization software and data mining or data modeling software, and the platform has to be tailored to the specific demands of the project. The information delivery we need can't just be in the form of static reports; rather, we must build an interactive type of analytics from the "dashboard" level all the way down into specific pieces.

The dashboard is usually an interactive repository of information for the user, and it should be relevant to whatever the user manages on a regular basis. The aim is to provide users with tools that offer multiple ways to interface with the data, from a summary level down to the underlying details within any measurement or graph.

In reporting and analytics, it is important to take a "day in the life" approach in understanding the user. How will that user engage with the analytics on a day to day basis? Anticipate what questions the user will have. Think of how an inquisitive three-year-old asks an endless chain of "why?" questions to his or her parent. Similarly, for the user to engage with the data, the "whys" must be apparent at every level. For example, if a user sees a downward trend or a variance on a reporting dashboard, the next action would be to click on (drill into) that specific area and be presented with more detailed information that answers the "why." Then they can click again for the "why" that explains the first "why," and so on. This is what we refer to as information delivery design, and is just as critical as the cost and profitability calculations.

Next you have the profitability "engine" in the middle to collect all of the revenue data and do some of the profitability modeling around standard rate cost recovery, cost allocations, funds transfer pricing, and capital assignments (basically, importing customer revenues and banking balance items). In this way, we're creating what's called a performance management ledger. So, it involves designing a way to calculate profitability at the intersections of all the dimensions we talked about in chapter 5.

Following that, you have cost modeling, which is one of the biggest and most complex parts of the architecture. It requires an application that can model information from expenses all the way over to services, resources, and activities. This requires special planning around both methodology and technology deployment and must answer a bevy of interrelated questions. What exactly are the dimensions? Where are the data sources that are going to feed it? How are we going to manage the outputs? How do those outputs fit into the profitability system as a whole? How does all that translate into the reporting and analytics utilized by the user community? They're all pieces of the bigger puzzle.

Data management is yet another area. Both of these applications (cost modeling and multidimensional profitability) require tremendous amount of data that must be collected, categorized, and stored (in a data warehouse or a "datamart"). Data management consolidates all the various data inputs that are used across these applications to produce the overall solution. That data can include hierarchies, volume data, the financial data from the general ledger, information we may collect from cost studies across the organization, etc.

Finally, you have the contributors. One of the big questions of design and architecture involves executive governance. Who serves on those governance committees? Who are the big stakeholders? How are they going to make decisions? Which guiding principles will provide the rules of the road? Annual cost studies, core data sources, and technology support also round out the "contributors" component.

And at the end of the day, that massive structure makes up the blueprint or solution design for a functioning enterprise profitability management system or solution.

JUDGING A BOOK BY ITS COVER

Let's talk about the output—what we're actually delivering through design and architecture. Basically, we create what's called a "design book," in which we define, in detail, all of the data elements, information requirements, and reporting needs. The design book encompasses every dimension, every core source, every piece of data that constitutes the profitability solution.

A design book is a detailed list of dimensions, structures, fields, and data elements required for the analytics solution. It helps the business or finance team communicate with the IT or data teams on the specifics of each data element needed for the solution. It helps clarify the information needed by the user in relation to the specific data elements the IT team needs to capture. For example, if the user says they want to stratify profitability data by credit score, credit score becomes a required data element, and the data team would define the specifics of how and where that data will be sourced and provided to the profitability solution.

We're generating information to produce insights that lead to a profitable impact. The main objective is to define a sustainable solution design that concentrates organization resources on delivering *insight* and *impact* rather than just generating information, and this is where many organizations go awry.

COST AND PROFITABILITY ANALYTICS

Resource Commitment

Many implementations result in an unsustainable monthly production cycle that leaves minimal time and resources for value added analytics.

In these cases, monthly production cycles extend and end just prior to beginning the next monthly cycle, effectively limiting benefit realization. Thus, failing the business case for actionable profitability analytics and obstructing the ability to drive continuous improvement.

Keys to success:
! Enhanced Enterprise Engagement
! Sustainable Production Processes
! Effective Technology Automation

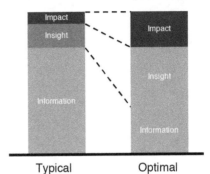

Monthly production and analytics time distribution

Typical   Optimal

Good design and architecture can shift resource time commitment from information production to value added analysis

Too often, the people running a data analytics program are caught up in a monthly cycle of doing nothing but producing information for information's sake. They're operating on a kind of *Field of Dreams* paradigm, where "If you build it, they will come"—if you collect the data, someone will find a way to use it. But the "Field of Dreams" logic means there's no strategic plan to take the information that is gathered and generate insights that'll have a profitable impact on the organization. It's building a beautiful, pristine baseball diamond—but Shoeless Joe and his pals never materialize out of the cornfield to come play on it.

The purpose of design and architecture is that it sets you up for success in deployment. It makes sure every element of the system is in place and has a clear purpose. There's a famous saying, dubiously attributed to Abe Lincoln—"If you give me four hours to chop down a tree, I'm going to spend the first three hours sharpening my axe."

Honest Abe never worked in profitability analytics, but his words of wisdom are apt. *Planning and preparation is everything.*

I've worked with clients who called me to rescue them from disastrous projects resulting from implementing without a good solution-design blueprint. They just started building without doing the upfront foundational elements. What ends up happening to such companies is they have to rebuild soon after launch. The lack of architectural foresight means it cannot deliver on the desired outcomes and basically collapses under the weight of its own complexity.

Recently, I helped a company out of this exact situation—the "ugly" case study I mentioned in Chapter 4 when I talked about the good, the bad, and the ugly. They had hired a Big Four consulting firm to build a profitability analytics module, instead of Armada. We lost the deal, but evidently made a lasting impression during the RFP process with our focus on design and planning. Three or four months into the implementation, they realized, "Hey, we haven't even really set a good design foundation." They had failed to do the upfront design, and they hadn't thought through the methodologies, guiding principles, or performed an honest assessment of their capabilities, and their data management was poor. They basically had fallen prey to all five of the common pitfalls. During the engagement, they called back and asked us to work with the competitor firm and get the project back on track. We obliged and executed on our design and assessment approach to right the ship.

Their mistakes and rushed implementation cost the company a year of lost work. A whole year to fail at getting things right. And when you're paying a Big Four consulting firm for a year, that's a pretty costly proposition. The value of thorough upfront planning and solution design cannot be understated.

If you're trying to build a house without a set of blueprints, it doesn't matter if you have the smartest people in the world on your team. You can't just wing it and hope for the best, or tell yourself that any problems will be fixed as they emerge. You need to have a design going in.

The way to develop the right design is by really looking at where you are now and where you need to be. The difference between those two points tells you what challenges you need to overcome first. That's the subject of Chapter 8, where I'll teach you how to assess your capabilities as an organization as you undertake the implementation process.

CHAPTER EIGHT

ARE YOU READY? ASSESSING YOUR CAPABILITIES

People often tackle major projects with the mindset that there is a clear division between "planning" and "doing." "Planning," according to the usual line of thought, precedes implementation, while "doing" is what happens when the planning is done and it's time to execute. However, in profitability analytics, planning *is* doing. Even during implementation, you're still conceptualizing and preparing for each step in the process before you deploy the program. Remember Abe Lincoln's adage? Hone the blade of your axe until it's razor-sharp. If you put in the preparatory work, the tree you're trying to chop down won't stand a chance.

Planning requires asking yourself the hard questions and honestly appraising your strengths and weaknesses as an organization. Actionable analytics needs the right environment to be sustainable over the long term. Once again, it's a journey, not a destination. And that's a journey you don't want to undertake aimlessly, wandering about with no compass, no map, and nothing but a few Snickers bars for sustenance. You want to have a clear direct path and foresee every obstacle you're going to have to overcome to get there, while marshaling the resources necessary to carry you all the way.

And what happens if you *don't* do your due diligence? You'll likely run into budget overruns and other organizational and logistical mishaps that could have been avoided. It really is so important to get it right the first time rather than trying to fix problems as they emerge. A rocky start is problematic because even if you somehow manage to patch things up on the fly, stakeholders have already started to lose faith in the program, before it has even gotten off the ground. And trust, once lost, is hard to win back.

This chapter details how to conduct a complete upfront assessment of strengths, weaknesses, and potential obstacles as you move into the implementation phase.

ASSESSMENT & GAP ANALYSIS APPROACH

Assessing impacts across primary solution components

The gap analysis approach evaluates current state capabilities against desired future state across the following primary solution components.

I Information – reporting and analytics desired from program

I Data – required data elements to fulfill information demands

I Methodology – changes necessary to profitability measurement methodology

I Process – impacts to recurring processes and production delivery

I Technology – evaluate the need for new applications or development changes

I People – impacts to various roles within the organization

Solution Components Assessment

Data

Information

Methodology

People

Technology

Process

THE SIX-STEP ASSESSMENT

Let's break down the assessment process into its discrete parts. Each of these is a minefield unto itself, containing risks that can derail the project or result in messy cost overruns and blown deadlines. But if you get these components right, you'll have a solid base from which to undertake deployment.

1. Information

Information is the lifeblood of a complex, collaborative venture of this type. The first step in assessing informational needs is to establish the "analytics inventory," also called a "reporting inventory." The analytics inventory identifies all of the reporting and analytics requirements of the various users. What is it that we want the users to be able to see? What do we want them to do with that information, and how will it add value to the organization? What are the gaps in the current state of information? How are the users making decisions in the absence of this information? What decisions would be made differently when we provide the data, and would those decisions improve profitability? If users had better information in a timelier manner, would it foster profitable growth? By answering these questions, we can start to create a gap analysis to determine what we need to do to reach our target.

Moreover, in this step, we start to prioritize things by the value of the information and the value of that delivery, against the benefit or the cost of the delivery, against the benefit of the information. For example, one of our banking clients wants to evaluate the profitability of their current book of business with a customer while putting together a new deal with that customer. Without profitability analytics, they would need analysts to pull data from a variety of sources, collect it in an Excel workbook, apply their own methods of calculating the customer's overall profitability, and then visit with the client to review and price a new deal, which would then be sent up for management approval. That cumbersome process could take weeks.

In contrast, with the new solution, the measurement of the current customer's profitability is viewable via the analytics tool. Thus the salesperson or banker can review it with the client and even incorporate the prospective new deal directly into the analytics, negotiating different pricing scenarios while getting immediate feedback on the impact it will have on the overall profitability profile of that customer. This accelerated process is a boon for all parties: the customer can get the best prices without having to shop around, and the salesperson reduces his risk of losing the business due to a protracted deal-making process.

Assessing the information demand, the intended use, and the value the information provides establishes the backbone of the solution design and blueprint.

2. Data

The greatest methodology in the world is useless without the data to power it. It's like trying to drive a Ferrari with just a few drops of gas in the tank. And if data is the new oil, as the saying goes, then actionable profitability analytics is the refinement of that oil into a high-octane gasoline that drives more profitable business behaviors. It is important that we collect, manage, and refine the best data for providing actionable information.

In this part of the assessment, we consider which data elements we need to capture, and where we have gaps. In many companies, the data is already physically present somewhere, it just hasn't been organized or optimized yet. We need to process it so that it's ready to be fed into the analytics program to produce actionable insights.

The right data is contingent on the right dimensional hierarchy structures (which we talked about in Chapter 5), whether it's customer hierarchy, product hierarchy, organization hierarchy, etc. You can't find out the profitability of a product when you haven't defined the product and its relationships. All the different dimensions that comprise multidimensional profitability analytics—all the facets of the Rubik's cube—require corresponding data elements. If you can't measure it, you can't manage it.

When assessing the data necessary for profitability analytics, we focus on the following aspects:

1. Ability to collect from the best source: can we automate the collection of the required data or do we have to mine it manually? Is it readily available in a data warehouse or another systemic source?

2. Quality and credibility of the data: is the data validated as a quality source that would produce credible information for the users?

3. Frequency of update necessary for timely delivery: how often is the data reliably updated, how does that update frequency impact our own sustainability or guiding principles?

The core dimensions that companies want to measure in profitability analytics are customer, product, organization, and salesperson. Additionally, dimension data on customer segments, regions, channel usage, credit score, and other demographics about a customer are feasible and should be integrated into profit analytics. The more dimensional data is available to power the profitability models, the more insights we can gain, and the more valuable the analytics. This data collection and organization efforts required for profitability analytics can be challenging and complex, but the view is well worth the climb.

3. Methodology

Throughout Section II, we talked a lot about how guiding principles and good governance form the basis for methodology. In the implementation phase, "methodology" means zooming in from that 10,000-foot view and getting more concrete and ground level with calculating all the metrics that influence the process. How will you assign costs? What will be the key performance metrics for different financial areas to be examined? How will you measure return on risk-adjusted capital? All the different pieces of the financial mosaic depend on the right methodology for how you're going to calculate them, so that you can composite the many pieces into a coherent, cohesive picture.

4. Process

"Process" entails thinking through what the analytics program is going to look like every month or every quarter, figuring out how it's going to operate logistically, and assessing what resources (human, financial, technical, informational, etc.) you need to keep the wheels turning. Some companies overestimate their ability to sustain a big analytics program and end up biting off more than they can chew. If you're a top-ten bank and you only have three finance people dedicated to overseeing that program, that's not going to be sustainable.

Processes are closely linked with people (which, as I'll talk about in a moment, is the most crucial single element), which means making sure the right people engage in the right actions in the right order to execute on a continual, repeatable basis.

5. *Technology*

One of the challenges is balancing technical elegance with practical solutions. There are a variety of different tools and technologies that we can use. Evaluate the technology that permits you to implement your design, deliver vital information, manage the appropriate size and amount of data, and empower the people you've put in place to do their jobs.

The key with technology is, as we noted in the discussion on project pitfalls, that the solutions must be tailored to the problem at hand. Utilize technology that works for you, rather than trying to cram a proverbial square peg into a round hole.

There are four primary functions demanded by these kinds of analytics, and each function can require different technology applications:

- *Unit cost modeling application:* an activity-based cost modeling application used to model expenses into meaningful unit cost data;

- *Cost recovery/profitability application:* a profitability modeling application used to calculate high volume transactional cost data, manage detailed revenue and profit measures, and aggregate analytics through multiple dimensional structures;

- *Business intelligence/analytics delivery:* a reporting and analytics environment capable of developing reporting, dashboards, and analytics cubes, with large data volumes across a broad user community;

- *Data management/data quality:* applications that can manage large volumes of data and provide business users the ability to manage and monitor data quality issues within supporting data.

6. People

The central component of assessment, the hub of the wheel that holds it all together, are *people*. You simply can't do it without the right people in place.

It's not just about staffing the project with employees who have the right skillset (though that's of course important). It's also a matter of *change management*. This is a big project that's going to involve a lot of people, and it's going to impact their day-to-day work life. Change management in an analytics program requires acclimating people to a different way of doing things. You must help them to evolve past the long-held accounting-focused view of corporate finance and towards an altogether different paradigm that looks at the underlying economics of a business.

THE MOST IMPORTANT BUT OVERLOOKED COMPONENT
Many organizations fail to establish a clear strategy for change management

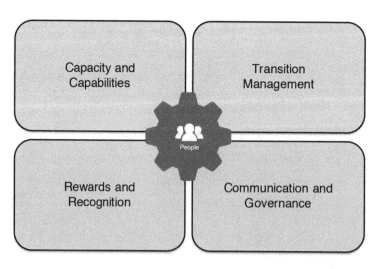

Another issue within change-management is determining how to measure performance and handle rewards and recognition. For example, will your employees' commission pay be based on "old" metrics, or will it be determined by the new analytics? (Recall the example from Chapter 4 on the company that used profitability analytics to modify its commission system, so as to drive more profitable behavior among its sales team.)

Remember that when it comes to change at work, people's first thought is, "How does this affect me, my job, or my compensation?" People reflexively resist any change that impacts their livelihood.

With profitability analytics, these change challenges are amplified. We are providing the organization the ability to model, measure, and manage financial performance in every nook and cranny of every department with detailed precision. And every insight generated has the potential to impact some aspect of people's jobs, and potentially their compensation, especially performance-based incentives.

We like to believe the rosy view that every one of our employees is a good corporate steward, actively working to foster the corporate values, mission, and profitable performance. But the fact is that "missions are the words hanging on walls, performance happens in the halls."

My twenty-five years of experience in navigating the halls and cube farms of some of the largest corporations has shown me how organizations are filled with underperformers, needless bureaucracy, and self-motivating behaviors. Yet, somehow, corporations squeeze out a profit, thanks largely to a handful of corporate champions and high-performing individuals who make up the slack. This is the greatest challenge of performance management, as good people are hard to find, harder to keep, and the underperformers are the most resistant to change.

So, these are the kinds of human-capital issues you must assess before hitting the big red LAUNCH button. You (the executive) and they (the people ultimately responsible for rolling out the program) must fully grasp the depth and complexity of what you're trying to do and make sure that everyone has what they need to go the distance. And make sure that if there is something they lack now (whether it's knowledge, resources, or technology), you will help them acquire it. Otherwise, the project will be on shaky ground when it launches.

Ironically, while "people" is the most important component, it's also the most overlooked. Project teams are so focused on the information, data, methodology, processes, and technology that they kind of miss the forest for the trees, neglecting that people are going to be the ones *using* the analytics. Training, communication, and change management are considered softer disciplines of project management, and when faced with tight deadlines, budgetary pressures, and other challenges, people management concerns tend to get dismissed or marginalized.

If we don't establish a clear vision for how we're going to change the organization and be transformational with these profitability analytics, then we've lost half the battle upfront. It's just another fancy source of information for people to look at and beat their chests about but not actually do anything with.

You can't take the people out of the equation. "It's business, it's not personal," the saying goes. But in this case, business *is* personal. At the end of the day, actionable profitability analytics is all about driving profitable behaviors and encouraging better decisions. That's something that occurs at the level of people. They're the alpha and omega of the whole thing.

MIND THE GAP: ASSESSMENT AND GAP ANALYSIS

There's no great mystery to conducting a gap analysis. The best approach is straightforward and methodical: look at each component, define its purpose, and state its corresponding deliverable.

ASSESSMENT & GAP ANALYSIS APPROACH

Project Framework

Our assessment and gap analysis approach evaluates various deployment current capabilities against desired future state outcomes and target state solution design.

The effort is focused on identifying gaps across the primary solution components early in the project and providing recommendations for future improvement. Gaps identified are included in a delivery roadmap for assigning resolution work efforts.

This comprehensive analysis provides a clear understanding of the challenges, capabilities, and capacity to deliver on time and on budget.

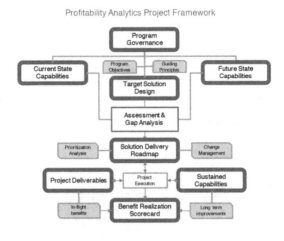

Profitability Analytics Project Framework

For each of the six components (data, information, methodology, process, technology, and people), we set up working sessions with the corresponding experts in each category and come up with an analysis that addresses 1) the leading practices in the industry, 2) the current state for that component, 3) the target state vision (where do we desire to be), and 4) the roadblocks that need to be overcome in order to get there.

It's all contingent upon the overarching objectives of the client. When those objectives are clear, we can prioritize what are the first things we need to address and start kicking off those initiatives.

MATURITY MODEL
Evaluating current and target state capabilities for each strategic component

	Lagging	Limited
	Basic Top Down Costing with Simple GL Based Allocations	Basic Activity **Based Costing Concepts applied as cost accounting**
Information	- Organizational GL based reporting - Supports macro LOB & legal entity - 'Below the line' indirect allocations not valued for business decisions	- LOB profitability with directional customer or product analytics - Functional operational cost data - Multiple sources of disparate cost reporting across enterprise
Data	- Primarily GL sourced - Spreadsheet based driver collection - Financial accounting inconsistencies challenge modeling efforts	- Drivers rely heavily on management estimates or static volumes - Minimal enterprise data governance - SCM considered in GL data governance
Methodology	- GL based allocations of indirect expenses, limited use of unit costs - Proxy drivers and macro cost pools with limited operational detail - Limited transparency & traceability	- Fully absorbed unit cost modeling - Supply based ABC model, unit costs vary significantly throughout the year - Limited enterprise visibility and traceability of source cost contributions
Process	- Manually intensive monthly process - Finance role limited to providing information, minimal analysis - Reactive governance for modeling methodology updates	- Utilizing ABC technology to produce monthly allocations and reporting - Significant work effort required for collecting and transforming data - Managed model release schedule
Technology	- Spreadsheet modeling for GL based allocations - Offline, ad hoc reporting & analysis - Users have limited access to underlying cost model data	- Invested in ABC technology application - Use of relational databases for data management - Disparate BI technologies used across Corporate & Business Lines
People	- Fragmented finance staff responsibilities - No formal training of finance staff - Management culture does not engage	- Dedicated but understaffed SCM team - Technology centric training available - Some accountability for indirect costs

Legend: Current State Assessment | Target State Design

MATURITY MODEL
Evaluating current and target state capabilities for each strategic component

	Leading	Advanced
	Integrated **Activity Based Costing Models** applied as business economics	Predictive **ABC Model Integrated with Planning and Profitability System**
Information	- Fully integrated into multi-dimensional profitability analytics - Business users leverage standard unit cost information for analysis - Finance governs one central source	- Unit cost information used in planning and forecasting - Predictive analytics and scenario modeling capabilities - Effective marginal pricing analytics
Data	- Business data warehouse integration - Automated data collection and ETL - SCM integrated into data governance - Cost fact data cubes available to users	- Fully integrated with core source systems and HR data - Unit costs data integrated into scorecard systems
Methodology	- Multi-dimensional unit cost modeling - Aligned with economics of business - Segregation of consumption based costs and business sustaining costs - Majority of costs are recovered with consumption volume drivers	- Ability to distinguish cost variability with reasonable actionability - Model architecture organized around company strategy, accountability, and ongoing governance - Adoption of performance sub-ledger
Process	- Finance role shifted to value added analysis instead of production - Defined cost study process as part of annual planning exercise - Established formal governance structure	- Focused effort on opportunity analytics - SCM team driving benefit realization and continuous improvement - Cost management and modeling distributed across enterprise
Technology	- Utilizing most capabilities of advanced ABC software - Integrated with enterprise BI analytics and reporting technologies - Integration into Customer analytics	- Sustainable automation of cost systems within overall business architecture - Application of statistical programs across customer profitability analytics
People	- Fully trained and resourced SCM team with dedicated IT Support - Collaborative management and accountability of indirect costs	- Cost group integrated with business analytics and process reengineering - Management culture fully embraces SCM program as strategic asset

Legend: Current State Assessment   Target State Design

As the assessment roadmap starts coming together, we can construct a "maturity model" that demonstrates what we have/can do, what we lack/can't do, and what we need to change in order to progress. We compare an organization's capabilities on each of the solution components to characteristics of other organizations. For each component, we assign a level of readiness, from "lagging" to "advanced." Note that not every company needs to (or even should) strive for the highest level on the chart. It really depends on their unique profile and strategic business needs. In some cases, it's enough to aspire to the "limited" or "functional" stages. Don't chase the "advanced" level just because a competitor down the street is doing it.

An example of this was the aforementioned bank that had been looking at outsourcing to lower costs. In that case, we determined that an "advanced" degree of capability wasn't needed; it would have been overkill, since that company's problem was limited in scope, related to cost takeout site comparisons and exception processing. They had a very specific, immediate need that was solved by a "lower" level of capability.

As I write this, I'm on the road working closely with a client company that *is* seeking those top-level, advanced capabilities. Our time frame is three years. In the profitability analytics field, the old saw about "slow and steady wins the race" is fundamental. For this company, trying to get there all at once, instead of over a longer timeline, would have been inadvisable: it would be extremely costly, logistically burdensome, and fraught with risk (since the more you hurry things, the likelier it is that the project hits a snag or some critical feature is overlooked.)

You can't rush a good thing. Thing big, start small, and deliver incremental value. Advance in discrete steps, from lagging to limited to functional to advanced. The patient approach pays off in the long run, and done correctly can provide the incremental value that self-funds the entire program.

The following graphic is another visualization of how Armada approaches the gap analysis for a hypothetical client. This chart is useful for demonstrating what you need to do to go from Point A to Point B to Point C.

Each of the "wedges" represents the six core components of assessment, and the concentric rings signify the ascending degree of maturity from lagging (innermost; red) to advanced (outermost; blue). The more opaque colors represent the *target* state; the bolder colored wedges show the company's *current* state.

The key takeaway here is that different components might be at different levels of maturity. Not all components have to move in sync. This gives the project greater flexibility in its goals and development.

MATURITY MODEL

Radar chart of initiatives to advance SCM Maturity Level

Program Initiatives

1. Increased Transparency
   One central source of transparent cost and profitability analytics accessible to all finance users

2. Customer Profitability Analytics
   Enterprise data coverage of customer account profit measures, dimensions, and volumes

3. Consumption Based Methodology
   Enhanced methodologies for multidimensional cost modeling on a consumption basis with cost variability attributes

4. Sustainable Solution Processes
   Efficient processes for cost studies and modeling with effective governance on methods and data

5. Improved Modeling Technologies
   Upgrade technology infrastructure of modeling applications; Acumen Cost Analytics and Accord Profitability Analytics

6. Shared Accountability
   Collaborative engagement across finance for cost analytics as a shared strategic resource

Initiatives to advance maturity levels

Lagging | Limited | Leading | Advanced

◁ - Program Initiative & Risk Assessment   Bold Ring = current | Shaded Ring = target

So in this case, "process" and "technology" were lagging, "information" and "data" were limited, and "methodology" was functional. The company only had to reach the functional level in "people," "process," and "technology." But for "methodology," they had to jump from functional to advanced. And so on.

HOW THE TORTOISE BEATS THE HARE

The first question execs usually ask me is, "What can we do to get started?" People always want to rush; they want to get into the action and don't want to do the planning. When it comes to the project timeline, everybody wants it done yesterday. But there's no shortcut: design, architecture, assessment, and gap analysis must come first. And every discrete step requires a thorough, methodical progression through the four Ds: discover, design, develop, and deploy.

It's just like in the famous fable: the plodding tortoise beats the overeager hare in the long run. It can be challenging, painstaking even, to move incrementally from one step to the next, but it's the only way to do it right and make it sustainable. Slow and steady wins the race. There's a lot of moving parts and if you don't take care of all of them, the whole thing is likely to fail.

The next chapter will expand on the discussion of change management by looking at some (literally) battle-tested strategic approaches to unleashing complex projects, and examining how to manage people in a way that keeps the project moving forward.

CHAPTER NINE

"INSTANT THUNDER": DEPLOYMENT STRATEGIES AND NAVIGATING CHANGE

When Saddam Hussein invaded Kuwait in 1990, it caught the world off guard. The United States and its allies had to scramble to come up with a counter-strategy that would expel the Iraqi military from Kuwait while avoiding a bloody, protracted ground war.

Today, if you asked somebody who led the first Gulf War, they'd probably name guys like Norman Schwarzkopf or Colin Powell, but the lesser known Colonel John Warden III was arguably the most important architect of the US-led military campaign, and Operation Instant Thunder—the devastating air blitz he designed, which crippled Iraq's command and control centers in a matter of weeks—remains a valuable lesson for strategists in any field.

As an enthusiast of military history myself, as well as a strategy-minded CEO, Warden's vision has been an immense influence on me. His brilliant and battle-tested theories in his book *Winning in FastTime,* actually have a lot to teach us about how to successfully deploy a profitability analytics program.

Following his retirement from the Armed Forces, Warden consolidated his ideas into a comprehensive strategic protocol called the Prometheus Process. It's easily adapted to transformational business programs to rapidly manage change and execute with "speed to value." The Prometheus Process is based on the following principles:

- *Specific actions affect a specific future,*

- *every action takes place within a system of some kind,*

- *all systems have inertia and resist change,*

- *all systems have "centers of gravity" or leverage points of varying influence and control,*

- *change occurs when the "centers of gravity" are impacted to influence our future state desired outcomes,*

- *and impacting multiple centers of influence and control simultaneously will accelerate the change.*

In plotting the air campaign against Iraq, Warden viewed the enemy not just as a "military" or a "nation-state" but as a *system*. All systems also have a center or centers of gravity—different leverage points that exert varying levels of influence and control. The central tenet of the Prometheus Process is that if you can concentrate your assault on those points and change those centers of gravity, then you can successfully change the overall system. And by changing the system, you achieve your desired outcome.

What I love about Warden's process is that it doesn't depend on a linear, sequential plan of attack (first we go after A, then we tackle B, etc.). Instead, it creates a delivery plan—a campaign—that strikes all of these centers of gravity at the same time, mounting overwhelming force that topples the "enemy" in one fell swoop.

That's how you have to view deployment for an analytics program of this magnitude. It requires simultaneous execution that targets all the centers of gravity, thus facilitating the change that's required in the organization long-term. Out with the old, in with the new!

If someone tells you, "Well, our finance department doesn't report analytics that way," that's because they're accustomed to some ingrained habit that's going to be difficult to change. Change is hard, as the saying goes—for individuals, but especially for collective, systemic bodies like corporations. (And it's harder still if it's a large, complex corporation.)

A second military-inspired framework that can guide your deployment is known as the OODA loop, conceived of by John Boyd, who was an Air Force colonel, like Warden III, as well a combat pilot and military theorist. The OODA loops posits that any process of execution follows an iterative cycle that consists of four stages:

1. Observe (what is going on?)

2. Orient (how does this impact me?)

3. Decide (what action to take)

4. Act (follow through on your decision)

Once you've taken an action, the loop continues: observe, orient, decide, and act again. Iteration with the OODA loop depends on speed: the faster you can navigate this cycle, the more likely you are to succeed. And the agility to perform multiple cycles in the same time frame will accelerate "speed to value."

Boyd's theory was originally designed to help fighter pilots prevail in dogfights, but, like Warden's Prometheus Process, it is equally formidable in other contexts, like when you're rolling out an analytics program and must make quick, decisive changes on the fly. Yes, even after the exhaustive planning you've completed, you'll still need to modify the analytics program after it's deployed.

A great delivery approach with an accelerated aggressive execution plan will enable organizations with minimal resources to achieve improbable outcomes.

GOING INTO BATTLE WITH A PLAN

Ultimately, if you can manage simultaneous execution of all the components (targeting all the centers of gravity at once), along with an iterative, OODA loop-inspired development that ensures you're staying on the right track, you can manage an execution that is rapid and decisive but also controlled and tactical.

Since a good change-management strategy hinges upon targeting the centers of influence, the first step is to identify what they are. Warden describes these as the Five Rings. On the battlefield, they are leadership, system essentials, infrastructure, population, and fielded military. Operation Instant Thunder was so effective in part because American air power was directed at all of these five rings (and, in particular, the leadership) all at once.

In business, the five rings of control include:

- Leadership (must possess a vision for profit analytics use and strategic governing objectives)

- Technology (quality data, leading applications, and credible and actionable information delivery are essential)

- Processes (intentional processes to drive more profitable behaviors and sustain a long-term program)

- Change agents (people who can solve specific problems early on while serving as change champions in the organization)

- User population (they need to understand how to leverage profitability information in daily activities)

CHANGE RESISTANT CENTERS OF INFLUENCE AND CONTROL

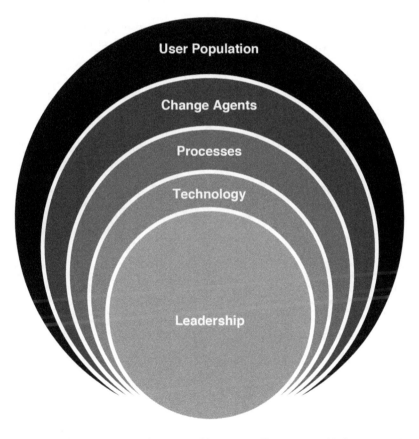

All organizations resist change and have specific centers of influence and control that defend against change. A successful deployment strategy will coordinate work efforts that move each center from a current state to desired future state in the shortest possible time horizon to ensure 'speed to value.'

First, leadership is, indisputably, a key center of gravity. When it comes time to roll out the program, we need to figure out how to effectively communicate and draw leadership into the process, so that they can be a champion throughout the organization for these improved analytics.

People in the corporate world are fond of talking about "executive commitment" as the key to success for any project. Sometimes that's used interchangeably with "executive involvement." But there's a distinction between the two. The former implies a greater level of participation, of bringing to bear one's strength as an executive or manager in committing to the program.

It's like a ham and eggs breakfast. The chicken was *involved*, but the pig was *committed*. Go whole hog and be the fully committed pig.

The second center of gravity is technology infrastructure: technology that delivers quality data and leading applications that can be leveraged to deliver profitability information to the broader user community.

Technology can be a barrier in a lot of these projects, because IT departments don't move as fast as we would like. They're used to doing things a certain way, so when you present them with a new approach, you're confronted with the organizational inertia that makes people resist change. Don't be surprised if the IT people tell you it can't be done the way you want it. That resistance is one of the barriers we must overcome decisively and quickly to make profitability analytics work.

The third ring consists of processes. There are a number of entrenched processes we must change, and it's not just the processes that we use to deploy actionable analytics. It's also the processes that are indirectly impacted by the analytics. For example, an actionable analytics program has recently been rolled out at a bank. A customer of that bank calls and requests that their overdraft fees should be waived because they're such a loyal customer.

With the changes brought about by the analytics program, now there might be a new process that guides decisions of this nature. Whereas in the past, the banker would grant or deny requests based on certain anecdotal metrics, or maybe intuition, or whether he happened to be in a good mood at the time, now that banker is following a different set of criteria. They can pull up the customer's profitability statement to make a fact-based decision on fee waivers, discounts, and other concerns.

We need to "conquer" old processes across the entire organization, looking at them through a gap analysis lens: What is the current state of those processes, what is our desired outcome, and what do we need to do to get from here to there?

The last two rings are more focused on navigating change. First, you have to work with your change agents or change champions, the people on the front lines who can get their colleagues to do things differently from now on. Usually, this is a business line executive who already knows what they want to do with the analytic capabilities, or it's a CFO for whom profitability analytics has long been at the top of their wish list—people who understand what these analytics do and grasp why they're important. They're the ones who will serve as ambassadors by convincing the broader community why the program is worthwhile while also helping to solve specific problems and remove obstacles that crop up after rollout. But basically, the goal is to leverage the change agents' expertise and their influence on the rest of the organization.

Finally, the last center of gravity is the end user population. It's imperative to clearly communicate what needs to be done for the user community to make sure the deployment succeeds. That might entail special training, for example. After all, the goal is *actionable* analytics: information to insight to impact.

CREATING A SHARED AGENDA

One of the biggest hurdles in deployment is bringing together factions of the organization in pursuit of a shared agenda on profitability. Some large organizations are divided into so many different divisions and departments that personal and departmental agendas interfere with "coalition building." In particular, there is a natural tension between profit-oriented front office operations and non-revenue-generating, back office cost centers. Therefore, one of our tasks is to bring these two groups together with a shared agenda. Ultimately, they're all part of one company and hence they're all pursuing the same overarching goal.

In a cost allocations environment, the back office is allocating the costs to the guys who produce the revenue, and of course they don't want any costs on the books because it starts to make them look unprofitable. The back office is preoccupied with controlling costs without limiting profitable growth. The front office is focused on maximizing profitability and achieving sustainable growth. Even though they're all working for the good of the company, there's a dissonance there, and this becomes more pronounced during deployment.

This kind of challenge—bridging the gap between departments and divisions—starts earlier in the process (we addressed it in Chapter 3 and Chapter 4). But it's also a deployment challenge, because even if you've established the proper set of guiding principles and guidelines to get everyone on the same page, you still have to create an engagement model in which you can get these factions to hammer out the details collaboratively.

We can achieve this by making the back office responsible for the unit cost being provided and the front office responsible for managing the volumes that are coming into the back office. The figure below shows the tasks both sides must undertake to meet each other in the middle.

When you achieve cost management/profit management harmony, you can effectively drive change in the organization and use that to optimize profitability.

ENGAGING THE ENTERPRISE ON PROFITABILITY ANALYTICS

Requires transparency, accountability, collaboration and actionable data

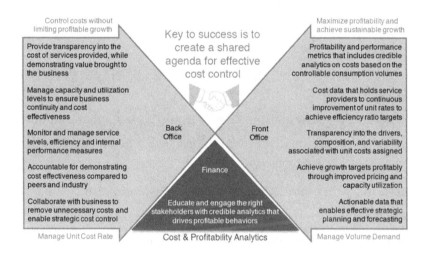

Note that the finance team occupies the middle. Finance's job is to educate and engage the right stakeholders with analytics that boosts profitable behaviors. But it can't do that effectively unless the cost management, back office side and the profit management, front office side are seeing eye-to-eye.

BACK ON OLD MACDONALD'S FARM (E-I-E-I-O)

Anyone who has managed a project understands that whether you succeed or fail depends on a lot more than the merits of the project itself. Never underestimate the human capacity for sabotaging a perfectly good idea! Group dynamics are hard to get right. Individual and collective human psychology plays a role. And for each of us, our individual capacity for logical analysis is more limited than we'd like to believe.

Human beings aren't robots. We're complex organisms driven by both reason and emotion. We like to *think* we're always rational, but the mind is very good at tricking us into believing that we're right and the other guy is wrong. None of us are perfectly rational 100 percent of the time. Even the smartest people in the room are just that, people—and people are inherently susceptible to cognitive biases.

Cognitive biases lead to false or irrational judgments. Common examples include the confirmation bias (the tendency to zero in on information that confirms our beliefs while overlooking contrary data), the belief bias (when our sheer conviction that our conclusion is right distorts our perception of the logical reasoning that got us there), or the outcome bias (putting too much weight on the *outcome* of a decision without critically analyzing the reasoning that produced it). Cognitive biases are especially tricky because not only can they lead us to the wrong conclusion but, by their very nature, they obscure the faulty logic that produced it. As I said, we human beings are good at deceiving ourselves.

Therefore, as you're rolling out the analytics program, you have to be aware that people will steadfastly defend their beliefs about cost and profitability, even if the data doesn't support those beliefs. They either have a distorted perception of what the deliverables and benefits are, or they have a defensive reaction to certain results that may not fit their perception of what's going on in their business. It's always easier for them to challenge the credibility of the modeling and the analytics than to accept that their own judgment is wrong.

Several years ago, I co-presented with a client at a large conference on bank profitability analytics. At these events, people always ask how to deal with this tricky situation. How do I handle executives who balk when the analytics aren't saying what they wanted them to say? My co-presenter had the best response in our presentation: the answer lies in just knowing how to deal with people. Remember the mnemonic E-I-E-I-O: *ego, interpretation, emotion, intelligence, optimization.*

Ego needs no explanation. People can be full of themselves and overconfident in their understanding of their business. They don't need any outsider telling them how to run it, and so they think the analytics should just be a tool to justify their instinctual decisions. The analytics data is going to produce many surprises, and bring about many changes, and this can be the blow to one's ego.

KEYS TO DELIVERING PROFITABILITY ANALYTICS TO STAKEHOLDERS

Take a deep breath and remember : E – I – E – I - O

Ego	• They know their business and don't need your help • Analytics are a tool to justify their gut instinct decisions
Interpretation	• Ensure managers understand the methodology, process and assumptions • There is likely some information they've always wanted that you can provide
Emotion	• Be prepared to defend results, especially when incentives are involved • The mere mention of unprofitable book of business gets strong emotions
Intelligence	• With Ego and Emotion in check, managers can think intellectually • Start analytical conversation that engages discussion <u>and</u> drives decisions
Optimization	• With managers engaged in analytics, demand for resources will grow • Minimize production efforts to enable solid preparation and analysis

The second part is *interpretation*. Make sure the managers understand the methodology and assumptions so that they can interpret the results correctly. In most cases, the information that the analytics program is now providing them is something they've always wanted—even if the data doesn't necessarily align with their expectations.

The other thing you must keep in check are *emotions*. Be prepared to defend those results, especially when incentives are involved, because emotions can run high and the mere mention of an unprofitable book of business can make stakeholders agitated and defensive.

However, once the stakeholders are able to grasp the results, and their egos and emotions are under control, they will start responding intellectually, rather than emotionally, to the business *intelligence* now at their disposal. They can engage in a rational, analytic conversation and start to migrate towards making more data-driven decisions, instead of operating on gut instinct or one-dimensional accounting data.

Optimization is when everything starts to crystallize. Stakeholders start implementing changes in response to the new information, and as they do, they can optimize the program based on new ideas and insights. This is the "tweaking" stage, when they can go back and refine methodologies or identify additional data points or other elements that will improve the process, making it more efficient for the finance team and more valuable to the organization as a whole.

Business *is* personal. As any executive knows, succeeding in the corporate realm is not just about facts and figures, balance sheets and spreadsheets, profit and loss and who is producing what revenue for whom, it's also plain old dealing with people. If you can't manage those relationships, empathize with stakeholders, and show that you understand that change can be difficult, it's hard to get the right results—even if you've done everything correctly up to this point.

WHAT WILL YOUR TOMORROW BE?

The best execution does not proceed in a linear fashion, tentatively moving from step one to step two to step three, but instead attacks the system's centers of gravity all at once. Once you knock out the "enemy's" defenses, you're in a good position to optimize—to refine and reform the analytics program once it's running.

Deployment is an area where your people skills will be key. Even with all the talk of guiding principles and governance, even if all the stakeholders have already agreed on the chosen methodologies and talked about what to expect after launch, the business intelligence that profitability analytics delivers may surprise them. And not everyone reacts well to surprises—especially if it reveals that their line of business hasn't been performing as well as they thought. Control egos, temper emotions, and help execs understand the new profitability and cost information and how to apply it. In turn, they will recognize the value of the program and accept that they must adapt to a new paradigm.

"To win, you must decide what you want your tomorrow to be, and then make it happen faster than the rate of change in your competitive environment," wrote John Warden III. Deployment is that shining moment when your dreamed-of tomorrow becomes your lived-in today. If you act decisively and marshal all the resources at your disposal, your "adversary" is sure to fall.

In the next chapter, we'll wrap up the lessons of the book, and look at how you can take the next steps to initiating an actionable analytics program in your own business.

CONCLUSION

THE VIEW IS WORTH THE CLIMB

I was seventeen years old, the age when young people on the cusp of adulthood start making real choices about their future, as they try to figure out their place and purpose in the world. This was long before I had even heard the term "profitability analytics." In fact, I was drawn to an altogether different field: education. I wanted to work as a teacher. I could see myself in a classroom, holding forth on some subject in which I was a self-assured expert, cultivating minds, conveying knowledge.

One morning, I casually mentioned this plan to my dad, who peered at me from over the newspaper and said, "Son, there's no way you're gonna be a teacher. You'll be broke for the rest of your life." And he instead pushed me to pursue a business degree, with a focus on accounting. Naturally, I reacted with the stubbornness with which any teenager reacts to his father's unsolicited advice, but I listened to his reasoning. He didn't pressure me or coerce me, but he did get me to look at things differently. In the end, I was persuaded.

I started college the following year as an accounting major, and that decision launched a career path that I never could have imagined.

Looking back, I'm ever thankful, because while teaching is a noble profession, finance and accounting was surely a better fit for me. But I never lost interest in teaching. In fact, my career arc has come full circle into my personal passion for teaching. One of the things I most enjoy is educating others. And I'm so grateful that my experience and my position as a CEO of Armada enables me to teach some brilliant individuals at some of the best companies the concepts and practices we've discussed in this book.

WHERE WE'VE BEEN, AND WHERE WE'RE GOING: A SUMMARY

In Section I, we compared GAAP with cost and profitability analytics and looked at some of the advantages the latter has over the former. We also examined the importance of *transparency:* having one centralized source of information for all stakeholders to work from—one version of the truth. Section II was all about methodology: setting up clear guiding principles as the "guardrails" that keep the project from being driven off a cliff. Guiding principles are not the same as methodology, but they do provide a basis for methodology to emerge. You need these principles to establish objective criteria about how to measure and manage, instead of just deciding who's right or wrong based on who shouts the loudest or makes the most noise or pulls the right strings.

Section II also provided an overview of the specific methodologies. Multidimensional profitability analytics provides a Rubik's Cube-like 3D model of a company's financial performance. Strategic cost modeling unveils the causal drivers of expense in the enterprise.

Both offer a window into the underlying economics of the company's unique business model, providing fresh insight that impacts the bottom line.

Section III was all about the "think big, start small, deliver incremental value" approach to implementation. It's not something you can rush. It must be planned meticulously, even when you're champing at the bit, rearing to start. I get it. But slow and steady wins the race.

When it's finally go time, you want to tackle the problem with the strategic acumen and tactical execution to ensure victory. We discussed implementing with military precision to deploy changes in the company that engage decision makers with analytics that drive more profitable business behaviors. That's the blueprint for success and a proven path to benefit realization.

HOW TO GET STARTED

The arduousness of undertaking an analytics program is not easily evident from the eye-candy charts and slick presentation visuals that are often a company's first introduction to the field. And that's why I have striven to give you an honest sense of the down-and-dirty work involved in deploying profitability analytics via this book. Failure is a likely outcome for the underprepared and underinformed. But the biggest failure is the "failure to launch"—to not do it at all, because the strategic and financial utility of these analytics is undeniable.

Until now, we've still been speaking mostly of foundational practices evolved from past experiences. But now, it's time to take the next steps for your journey into profitability analytics.

Most common pitfall: Failure to Launch

Demonstrating value before major investment gains executive <u>commitment</u>

Solve a problem first

- Gain interest by demonstrating value in a specific area of concern
- Prototype methodologies as proof of concept (POC) project

Build a proven business case

- Quantify benefit realization from POC and seek champions
- Build business case as a self funding program

Develop an iterative approach for rollout

- Establish a roadmap based on prioritized benefit opportunities
- Think big, start small, and deliver incremental value

The first step is intuitive: identify a problem that profitability analytics can solve. In a large, complex company, there are many problem areas that make good candidates for a starting point, so which do you pursue? I advise tackling a big problem first. It's like the law of the playground: if you go after the biggest, meanest bully and knock him flat, then *you'll* be on top. After that, the other bullies are small potatoes by comparison.

This first problem you take on should serve as your proof-of-value or proof-of-concept project, addressing one area of the organization in a way that illustrates how these analytics can be applied to other problems too. It encourages executive commitment for enterprise deployment when you can deliver something quickly out of the gate.

And then you can use that to build a proven business case for enterprise-wide implementation. You can start to quantify the expected benefit realization. Soon, the head of every department will be clamoring for analytics implementation in their line of business too.

It's important to generate benefits as soon as possible. That doesn't mean rushing the process. It doesn't mean cutting corners. It doesn't mean forgoing the necessary planning. It just means achieving tangible value early on rather than waiting one to three years until the whole program is "complete."

Finally, once you've solved that initial problem for which you can show real value and build a persuasive business case, don't try to boil the ocean. Build an iterative approach across the enterprise so that, with every iteration, you're solving a new problem based on a clear roadmap that lets you knock out the bullies as they come along.

TWO OUT OF THREE DENTISTS RECOMMEND IT

Most of the examples and case studies in this book have focused on the banking industry, since banks make up the bulk of our clients, but profitability analytics are applicable to virtually any field. After all, profitability is the universal benchmark for corporate health in every industry. All businesses have customers. All businesses have sales people. All businesses have back office and front office operations. All of them involve a bevy of interrelated, interlocking dimensions that turn this way and that like the rows and columns on a Rubik's cube.

I took my son for a dental appointment the other day, and the dentist and I got to chatting. We ended up having lunch afterwards, and I explained a little more about what I do and how I help the companies that hire me. He was amazed by how applicable these analytics are, even to a small business like his. "In the healthcare field, I have all these different procedures, and from a business standpoint, not all of them are created equal," he explained. "Some cost a lot, some cost a little. Some bring in a ton of money, and others don't.

But it's hard for me to determine what's what." He saw the value of what profitability analytics could do in terms of demystifying all these different product and service offerings and allow him to make better strategic decisions about how to grow his business.

His small family dental practice is different in every way from the major international banks I usually consult with. But fundamentally, the concepts are the same. Now, whether he can afford me is a different question! But it was an illuminating conversation for both of us nonetheless.

Actionable profitability analytics could transform your organization too.

I'm grateful to be a trusted business advisor to some prestigious organizations, who have taken a chance on a boutique firm like Armada, choosing us with this major undertaking over some of our larger, household-name competitors. And I'm very grateful that they've remained great clients throughout the years.

One of the great sources of satisfaction in my line of work is that we can actually quantify the value that we bring to the organization. In cost and profitability analytics, we can measure the benefit of our work very precisely. In fact, it's the essence of what we do. And it's exciting to stay in touch with client companies for years, even after the formal business relationship has concluded, and hear about the brilliant things they've done with the analytics we helped them put in place.

I'm also grateful for having a team of people who learned the art and science of profitability analytics and share as much passion as I do about this admittedly nerdy subject. Several members of our team have been with me for years, some straight out of graduate school, and since then, they have become stalwarts. Together, we've built Armada into the highly regarded company that it is. Our people eat, breathe, and sleep these analytics and they're constantly thinking of how to push the envelope and expand what we can deliver.

This is a personal and professional passion of mine. I love connecting with people and championing their efforts to improve the profitability of their organizations. I love to do workshops for client teams and come in and really talk through what they could expect, what they could do. I welcome the opportunity to meet, connect, and teach in more details these topics to help improve the financial performance of every organization.

You have to believe in what you teach, and I believe in the value of profitability analytics with the fervor of a street corner preacher. It's not a belief born out of blind faith; it's quantifiable. The proof is in the numerical pudding.

Doing it is tough—that's one of the themes we've been driving home in this book. It's no walk in the park; it's a long hard slog to the top of K2, and you can't get there by rushing, or you'll be spent by the time you reach base camp. But if you put the work in, plan carefully, and follow a proven methodology that we at Armada have been perfecting for decades, you'll arrive at the summit. And from there, believe me: the view is worth the climb.

Thank you for taking the time to read *Actionable Profitability Analytics*. I have spent my entire career in this niche field of finance and the last several months trying to condense that experience into this book. If you are interested in diving deeper into profitability analytics for your company, please visit our website, **ArmadaConsulting.com**, for more tools, tips, or accelerators to launch your project. For speaking engagements or training workshops, please email me at **info@ArmadaConsulting.com**. I hope you enjoyed the read and look forward to hearing about your success.

Connect with me on LinkedIn at
https://www.linkedin.com/in/sswise/.

ABOUT ARMADA

Armada was established in 2002 with one focused mission: *to improve the performance and profitability of every organization we are privileged to call client.* We bring together talented professionals, proven solutions, and advanced technologies into a results-oriented practice that achieves measurable profitability improvements.

OUR SERVICES

Consulting & Advisory

- Management consulting focused on FP&A function
- Leading practice methodology training
- Industry research and analysis

Software & Solutions

- Acumen Cost Analytics
- Accord Profitability Analytics
- IBM Analytics, Oracle, and SAS integrations

Services & Support

- Managed Service Solutions
- Technical Implementation Services
- Production Support Services

CPSIA information can be obtained
at www.ICGtesting.com
Printed in the USA
LVHW082344250719
625403LV00002B/2/P